Comparing American and British Legal Education Systems

Comparing American and British Legal Education Systems

Lessons for Commonwealth African Law Schools

Kenneth K. Mwenda

CAMBRIA PRESS

Youngstown, New York

Library of Congress Cataloging-in-Publication Data

Mwenda, Kenneth Kaoma.
Comparing American and British legal education systems: lessons for Commonwealth African law schools / Kenneth K. Mwenda.
p. cm.
ISBN 978-1-934043-51-6 (alk. paper) 1. Law schools—Accreditation—Africa, English-speaking. 2. Law schools—Accreditation—Great Britain. 3. Law schools—Accreditation—United States. 4. Law—Study and teaching—Africa, English-speaking. 5. Law—Study and teaching—Great Britain. 6. Law—Study and teaching—United States. I. Title.

KQC48.M84 2007
340.071'141—dc22

2007001806

For my admirable son, Joseph T.K. Mwenda II,
whose arrival in the family is divine inspiration,
filled with truth and virtue,
and whose unconditional love and affection
continue to be an uplifting blessing.

Contents

List of Tables and Figures

FOREWORD

Drawing on his rich scholarly experience as a former academic in the UK and in Commonwealth Africa, and informed by his wide professional experience as an international attorney in the US, Dr. Kenneth K. Mwenda, provides a first-class treatment of important and salient policy issues underpinning the development of legal education systems in the US, the UK and Commonwealth Africa. The author has succeeded in answering vexing and elusive questions that have preoccupied several discussions by law students, law professors and other interested commentators, regarding such hot topics as the difference in standards between an undergraduate first professional law degree and a graduate first professional law degree.

Throughout the book, the author has been able to sustain his thesis intelligibly, arguing that although the UK and the US have fairly old and well established universities, a number of LLB programmes at Commonwealth African law schools are as good as similar programmes at leading British and American law schools—that is, the LLB degree in the UK and the JD degree in the US. By contrast, as the author argues, the LLM and SJD/JSD programmes in the US, unlike their UK counterparts, the British LLM and the British PhD in law, do not have much to offer to Commonwealth African law schools (i.e., law schools in countries such as Botswana, Cameroon, Ghana, Kenya, Lesotho, Malawi, Namibia, Nigeria, Sierra Leone, South Africa, Swaziland, Uganda, Tanzania, Zambia and Zimbabwe).

In this book, the international and comparative analysis of various undergraduate and postgraduate law degree programmes in the UK, the US and Commonwealth Africa provides a novel and authoritative treatment of legal education systems in these parts of the world. Without doubt, the author has succeeded in raising challenging questions and offering solutions to such questions, regarding, for example, the troublesome duration of most postgraduate degree programmes at African universities. It should be added, however, that the criteria or methodology of ranking or judging academic degrees or law schools varies from context to context, and that the author is fully awake to such issues.

This book is certainly a valuable asset to a wide range of audiences, including prospective law students, current law students, law professors, many other academics and practising lawyers. The book provides a holistic and balanced treatment of an inherently contentious topic, setting out a strikingly frank and honest discussion of important policy issues in the development of legal education in the Anglo-Saxon world. The themes, issues and conclusions expressed by the author will, no doubt, give fruit to further debate on this topic. The author has succeeded in sowing seeds for critically insightful discussions from the readership.

All in all, the book is a well-written treatise, and the arguments advanced by the author are fully supported by extensive use of references. It will certainly be a valuable addition to the bookshelves and libraries of many universities and law schools, and everyone interested in the development of higher education will, no doubt, find this book a valuable piece of research work.

Zacharie Tamainot-Telto, PhD
Senior Research Fellow
University of Warwick, UK

Preface

There is a dearth of literature for law schools in Commonwealth Africa to consider when developing law degree programmes to meet challenges of the new millennium. And there is insufficient evidence of documented international and comparative studies examining intricate aspects of legal education in the US and other common law jurisdictions, such as the UK and some parts of Commonwealth Africa. This book endeavours to fill that gap.

The book is a sequel to an earlier refereed and scholarly journal article that I wrote a few years back, and whose citation is as follows: K.K. Mwenda, 'A new paradigm for Commonwealth African law schools: the decline of the LLB and PhD, and the ascent of the JD and SJD', *Journal of Commonwealth Law and Legal Education*, (Volume 3, Number 1, November 2004).

As law schools in Commonwealth Africa begin to confront the challenges of developing their legal education systems, so as to address contemporary issues in the law and development discourse pertaining to globalisation, they will, inevitably, face many issues that can only be best understood by reflecting critically, among other things, on how some developed jurisdictions have structured and grown their law degree programmes. To that end, should law schools in Commonwealth Africa simply imitate or transplant models of law degree programmes from abroad? And what lessons are there to follow? What should African students, based either on the African continent or in the diasporas, focus on when choosing law degree programmes at universities outside Africa? Are there any advantages in pursuing a postgraduate law degree programme in one country over the other or at one university over the other? What about league tables? How important are they? And what about the issue of accreditation of law schools and law degree programmes? Does that really matter? And are there any lessons to be learned?

By its very nature, the topic under investigation is unavoidably contentious, meaning that some arguments in the book may, understandably, strike a nerve or two. But it is not the aim of this book to cause trouble. That is far from it. Given the contentious nature of the topic, some arguments are likely to be misunderstood or may be met with some controversy or hostility. However, in dealing with a topic of this kind, the role of the author should not be understood as being confined merely to saying or writing only about things that are 'acceptable' in the eyes or ears of the public, or saying or writing about things for the sake of simply appeasing or pacifying the audience, but rather to tell the truth as it is, no matter how painful the truth may sound. In that sense, the book charts a new path that has not been trodden fully by published scholarship. An important caveat here is that the book explores a critical path that has, for some time now, occupied the minds of several educationists, and continues to dog several internet debates and discussions. Yet, most of these ideas have not been concretised into proper scientific and academic research. Many law students and prospective law students continue to debate and discuss the merits of pursuing graduate law studies in one jurisdiction over the other. But there are still very few convincing answers out there. This book, therefore, is an attempt to provide some responses.

While the book is not an indictment of any particular jurisdiction or law school, it offers an objectively balanced discussion, covering weaknesses and strengths of legal education systems in Commonwealth Africa, the UK and the US. The book weaves through all these jurisdictions, highlighting what one jurisdiction can learn from the other(s). The book argues, for example, that a factor that has contributed to the shaping of the landscape of legal education in Commonwealth Africa is the interpretation of law by the early judges, the civil servants and the academics in the newly independent African States. The book also explains how some academic programmes were constructed on the basis of the view of the world, as held by some expatriates.

Chapter One provides an introduction, highlighting the context of the study. The chapter identifies Commonwealth African jurisdictions that follow the Roman-Dutch law system in addition to the common law. The role of expatriate academics in developing legal education systems in Commonwealth Africa is also spelt out. The chapter examines the coming on board of indigenous African academics, including some developments leading to years of pioneer professorships and when African universities began to suffer from poor funding.

Chapter Two examines the primary university-level qualification to become a lawyer in the USA, the UK and South Africa. The chapter looks at how the Juris Doctor (JD) degree was introduced in the US, highlighting how some universities in jurisdictions outside the US, such as Canada, China and Australia, are beginning to pick up and transplant models of law degrees from the USA. A related issue here is the academic rank of the American JD degree, in relation to comparable law degrees. The chapter answers question such as, is a JD degree a Doctorate degree in the real sense, and how is the JD degree viewed by the legal community outside America?

Chapter Three examines post-JD qualifications in the US and the issue of their recognition. The chapter identifies the JD degree, instead, as the primary qualification to practice law and enter academia in the US. A question is then posed: what to do with the post-JD degrees from America? Disparities in academic standards on American LLM and SJD programmes are highlighted, raising serious concerns regarding the credibility of American LLM and SJD degrees.

Chapter Four examines the concept of accreditation of law schools and the accreditation of law degree programmes, highlighting, among other things, the issue of private and public universities and their accreditation. The chapter highlights also a notable shortcoming of the British PhD system, and proceeds to examine the concept of a *PhD by submission of published work*, the American *PhD by coursework and dissertation* and the concept of Higher Doctorates in the UK and the Commonwealth.

Chapter Five examines the role of university league tables, fleshing out pertinent issues that are often considered when formulating league tables. The chapter presents the Ivy League Universities and identifies some of the best ranked law schools in the US. Also, the Russell Group of Universities and some of the best ranked law schools in the UK are identified. Then, the chapter proceeds to discuss some financial dimensions of university league tables before culminating in a discussion of the ranking of universities in Commonwealth Africa. The chapter concludes with policy considerations surrounding the debate of whether or not to privatise university education in Africa.

Chapter Six is the concluding chapter. It sets out the main recommendations of the study to assist law schools in Commonwealth Africa in developing their law degree programmes.

Much of the book is informed by material available up to and including January 1, 2007. However, the interpretations expressed in the book, including any omissions or conclusions, are entirely mine and should not be attributed to any third-party or institution.

Acknowledgements

Now that the writing of the book is complete, I am faced with a task which is by no means easy to fulfil. I would like to thank my dear wife, Dr. Judith M. Mvula-Mwenda, and my admirable son, Joseph T.K. Mwenda II (to whom I have dedicated this book), for their unfailing love and support. I would also like to acknowledge the inspiration that I continue to draw from my dear parents, the late Mr. Joseph T. Mwenda and Mrs. Esther M. Mwenda. They both hold a very special place in my heart. And I cannot stop without thanking my many good friends, family members and professional colleagues whose names, if I were to list them all, would occupy a whole chapter in this book. I thank them all for their support and friendship over the years. I am also grateful to Cambria Press and to the peer reviewers for the excellent work leading to the publication of this book.

Chapter 1

Introduction

This book examines the extent to which Commonwealth African law schools should or could learn from experiences of American and British law schools in developing their own academic programmes. It examines degree programmes at American and British law schools with a view of determining whether Commonwealth African law schools should simply transplant models of university degrees from the US or the UK to Africa. Analogies are drawn from developments in Canada and Australia where some universities have now started to follow the US, abandoning the traditional undergraduate law degree programme, the Bachelor of Laws (LLB) degree, in preference to offering a post-Bachelors degree, the US-style Juris Doctor (JD) degree.

An underlying thesis of the book is that although the UK and the US have fairly old and well-established universities, a number of LLB programmes at Commonwealth African law schools are as good as similar programmes at leading British and American law schools—that is, the LLB degree in the UK and the JD degree in the US. The book argues that, by contrast, the Master of Laws (LLM) and Doctor of Juridical Science (SJD) programmes in the US, unlike their UK counterparts, the British LLM and the British PhD in law, do not have much to offer to Commonwealth African law schools. If anything, a number of American law schools are constructing *unaccredited* post-JD degree programmes, such as the LLM and SJD degrees, which Americans themselves often shun and do not even attach much value to, as a way of making easy money out of desperate foreign-trained lawyers who either want to break into the US job market or have limited knowledge and information on the US system of legal education and law practice. That said, the trend in the UK of permitting some LLB graduates to proceed directly to PhD programmes has limited attraction in Africa.

1.1 The Context of the Study

The book stands back from classroom pedagogy and avoids the polemics associated with the elaborate process of curriculum design. Neither does the book engage in pedantic issues of various syllabi of courses on university law programmes nor does it indulge in intricacies of teaching methods, such as the Socratic method of teaching law at most US law schools. What the book seeks to do, instead, is to provide, first, an international and comparative study of academic programmes at American and British law schools. Secondly, the book examines the issue of whether or not African law schools should adopt a particular Western model of academic programmes.

While the book focuses on prospects for the development of effective law degree programmes at law schools in Commonwealth Africa, it does not concern itself with similar or parallel issues in law schools of African countries that exist outside the Commonwealth. Reasons for this delineation are several. First, like the case of legal systems of Commonwealth African States that are based on the common law of England, the legal systems of African countries outside the Commonwealth are based on civil law systems of their colonial masters. Secondly, while the legal systems of Britain and most Commonwealth African States are common law based, the legal systems of other States in Africa and elsewhere outside the Commonwealth are civil law based. We are concerned with university degree programmes at law schools that follow the common law.

1.2 Commonwealth African Jurisdictions that Offer Exceptions to the Common Law

Within the Commonwealth, there are a few African countries, such as Botswana, Lesotho, Namibia, Swaziland, South Africa and Zimbabwe,[1] whose legal systems and jurisprudence are influenced primarily by the Roman Dutch Law system.[2] While the jurisprudence of most Commonwealth African countries follows the English common law, with some country specific adaptations to domestic legislation and judicial decisions, the jurisprudence of Botswana, Lesotho, Namibia, Swaziland, South Africa and Zimbabwe offer different variations. In these six countries, the influence of English common law is not as dominant as that of Roman-Dutch law. Although there are traces of English common law, say, in the company laws of these countries, Roman-Dutch law continues to play a significant part in the development of the legal systems of Botswana, Lesotho, Namibia, Swaziland, South Africa and Zimbabwe.[3] As Professor Iya observes:

> In the case of South Africa, the significant road marks in the historical path started unfolding in 1652 when Jan

> van Riebeeck arrived at the Cape and introduced Roman-Dutch Law, a European or Western legal system. At that stage, there were already black people present in South Africa who lived according to their own African legal system now popularly referred to as African Customary Law or Indigenous Law. In the early 1800s, the British took over the administration of the Cape from the Dutch and introduced and applied English law. This led to the influence of English law, although Roman-Dutch law continued to develop. That there would be a greater move towards English legal institutions is hardly surprising in view of the fact that the Cape became a British colony. Contact with and sympathy towards English institutions could only lead logically to greater contact with the English common law. Then arrived the Arabs, Indians, Christian missionaries, Jews etc., who introduced various religious laws: namely, Islamic, Hindu, Christian and Jewish law respectively. A fuller history of South African law provides dynamic intricacies of the development of the law, details of which need no further analysis here.[4]

According to Professor Iya,

> One often hears a statement like: the legal system in South Africa is Roman-Dutch law. This is not absolutely correct because as observed above, Roman-Dutch law forms only a part of the legal system of the country. English law also exercises its influence in its application especially to public law issues including legal institutions and the legal profession, just as much as customary law continues to influence the conduct of the majority blacks in South Africa. Therefore, it is more correct, when referring to the current legal system of the country as a whole that is applied, simply to speak of 'South African Law', a conglomeration of all the above different laws.[5]

While it is evident that the white South Africans inherited Roman-Dutch law from their ancestors in the Netherlands,[6] Botswana, Lesotho, Zimbabwe and Swaziland have almost no ancestral ties with the Netherlands and neither were they colonized by the Dutch. One can, however, understand easily that since Zimbabwe was under a racist white minority government prior to attaining political independence, Zimbabwe, like its neighbour, South Africa, embraced a type of jurisprudence that favoured the oppression of a black majority by white minorities. As a consequence, South Africa's legal system was a natural attraction to Zimbabwe. The racist Zimbabwe, as it was then, developed its legal system imitating developments in the legal system of the then apartheid South Africa.

In the case of Swaziland and Lesotho, these two countries have been geographical and economic enclaves of South Africa. Therefore, the transmission of legal values from South Africa to these two weaker neighbouring countries has progressed over a long period of time due, in part, to the sharing of some legal institutions[7] and to the geographical proximity of the countries. But more intriguing is the case of Botswana. Botswana lies further north of South Africa and is neighbours with Zambia. Yet, Botswana embraced Roman-Dutch law, although it lies further north from South Africa. Equally interesting is Namibia's case since, for the most part, Namibia was under German colonial rule. Yet, we see that from the time South Africa's Afrikaner-led National Party gained political power in 1948,

> ...Namibia exchanged one colonial experience for another. South Africa saw Namibia as, potentially, a fifth province for their country... In the late1950s and early 1960s, as in South Africa, the living quarters of black and coloured Namibians in towns were torn down. These residents, according to the principles of Apartheid, now had to be moved out of Windhoek city which was reserved for whites only or 'Slegs blankes' (a term that was to be used often in the years that followed). So-called 'coloured' Namibians were also to be divided

> from black Namibians. The task proved very difficult as the gene pool had been thoroughly mixed between all Namibians (white and black) since the time of the arrival of Europeans in the country in the early 19th century. Eventually, though, most 'coloured' Namibians in Windhoek where settled in 'Khomasdal', five kilometres outside of Windhoek, and the black population divided from 'Khomasdal' by a five hundred meter 'buffer zone' in what is known as 'Katatura'—which means '*a place where we don't want to stay*'. These so-called townships now form parts of Windhoek, and the buffer zones have been filled to connect these apartheid creations with the canter of Windhoek.[8]

A common denominator, however, linking Botswana to Swaziland and Lesotho, is that they all shared one regional university at some point, the multi-campus University of Basutoland, Bechuanaland and Swaziland.[9] And the development of legal education at this regional university could have been influenced by the more developed legal education system of the neighbouring South Africa.

1.3 Expatriates and the Development of Legal Education in Commonwealth Africa

Some factors that helped to shape the landscape of legal education in Commonwealth Africa included the intellectual interpretation of the law by the early judges, the civil servants and academics in the newly independent African States. At independence, most African States had very strong economies and these economies attracted professionals and academics from Europe, Asia and the US. Most of these professionals migrated to Africa not because they wanted to help Africans. A number of expatriates, especially the younger ones that did not have much work experience and decent qualifications, migrated to Africa partly because in their home countries they would not have found the right kind of jobs and they would not have earned themselves the respect that they quickly acquired in Africa. In the eyes of some of these expatriates, Africa was a breeding ground on which to gain valuable experience before returning home to Europe, Asia or America.

Also, the newly independent African States provided an opportunity for some of these expatriates to see the outside world for the first time in their lives. In Africa, the white expatriates enjoyed a good standard of living that they would never have dreamt of in their home countries. And today, we see that many academic programmes at African universities resulted from the in-put of some of these expatriate academics. Of course, it is not surprising that some academic programmes were developed on the basis of the expatriates' own view of the world and on the curriculum at the universities were these expatriates studied. That is not to say there were no credible and well-meaning expatriates in Africa. It is just that the category of credible and well-meaning expatriates consisted of a few individuals. In part, this is the history of the system of higher education in many parts of the Third World today.

1.4 The Coming on Board of Indigenous African Academics

As the economies of the newly independent African States began to crumble, expatriate academics started to leave. And the weakening of the post-colonial African economies gave reason for some expatriates to return to their home countries. Other expatriates were, however, not deterred by the deteriorating economic climate. They simply moved over to more prosperous African economies. However, as more expatriates left, a few indigenous African academics rose quickly to the ranks of associate and full professor, replacing the expatriates. This sudden 'professorial milestone' by some indigenous African academics was, in essence, a superficial way in which African universities tried to deal with the exodus of foreign academics while at the same time attempting to please the host government that African universities had succeeded in empowering blacks to senior academic positions.

Generally, unlike today, universities in many Commonwealth African countries enjoyed excellent government funding in the early years after political independence. And many African universities had in place well-funded staff development programmes on which they would send their junior academics abroad to undertake further studies. But, with the emergence of an elite group of indigenous African intellectuals, there was sudden urge for most African countries to Africanise academic positions in universities. It was, therefore, not uncommon to find senior academic titles of *professor* or *dean* being awarded dubiously to freshly graduated African PhDs who had not even served the academic community long enough and were far from being considered authorities in their fields. It must be observed that in many Commonwealth countries, unlike the US generally, the title of *professor* does not apply to any university or college teacher.[10] By contrast, the title applies only to those members of the academic community who have reached the pinnacle of academia and have gained wide recognition and respect amongst professional peers.[11] Other academicians are simply referred to as Lecturer, Senior Lecturer or Reader, as the case may be. As one instructive note points out:

> The meaning of the word *professor* (Latin: 'one who claims publicly to be an expert') varies. In most English-speaking countries, it refers to a senior academic who holds a departmental chair, generally as head of the department, or a personal chair awarded specifically to that individual.[12]

According to Wikipedia, in the US and Canada, 'unenlightened individuals use the term *professor* as simply a polite form of address for any teacher, lecturer, or researcher employed by a college or university, regardless of rank.'[13] However, it is important to recognize that in many other countries, to gain the title of professor, there is a huge milestone that very few people ever achieve.[14] In essence,

> The basic difference between levels of professor according to the national academic system is that in North America, the designation is based on career, whereas in Europe it is based on position. That means that if a North American *Assistant Professor* is performing particularly well, he or she can be promoted to *Associate Professor*, and if this is the case again, on to *(full) Professor* . In the European system, the different fields and sub-fields of teaching and research are allotted certain (professorial) *chairs*, and one can only become a professor if one is appointed to such a chair (which then has to be free, *i.e.*, unoccupied). Therefore, the different professorial ranks are not necessarily comparable.[15]

1.5 From Years of Pioneer Professorships to Years of Under-Funded Universities

The historical epoch in which freshly graduated African PhD holders began to ascend quickly to senior academic ranks of associate and full professor is what is referred to here as 'the years of pioneer professorships in Africa'. Parallel developments were taking place in the national economies of post-colonial African States. Their governments were busy nationalising strategic industries and placing the nationalised industries under the management of indigenous African technocrats and political appointees. Indeed, the years of 'pioneer professorships', like the years of nationalisations, were often a time riddled with notorious political overtones, especially where managerial, administrative or academic appointments were made solely on political grounds and consideration. Politics started entering academia.

Some indigenous African scholars that benefited from these 'pioneer professorships' were later able to work hard and publish enough peer-reviewed and respected work, thus attaining scholarly recognition internationally, while others failed to acquit themselves from the dubious 'professorships'. The latter group often ended up either as politicians or political appointees of some sort. Whichever way the pendulum swung, the university title of 'professor' was never abandoned even where the titleholder was no longer in academia and had since been appointed to government, or was serving as an elected member of parliament, or was pursuing other interests outside academia. It was hardly ever the case that such individuals were conferred the title of emeritus professor or any other unique professorial standing that would justify their continued use of the title professor even when they had already left academia. Even today, the university title of 'professor' is taken by many as a 'personal to holder' title, with its holders masquerading outside the realm of academia as 'the ever all-knowing and the ever all-wise'. However, unlike the period just after political independence, today's era is different and the title of 'professor' has to be earned genuinely and justifiably. It is certainly much more difficult now to earn the academic title and rank of professor in many decent African universities than it was during the years of pioneer professorships. A number of African pioneer professors would not have qualified as professors had they been evaluated using the standards that prevail today for professorial appointment at most decent African universities. Yet it is these same pioneer professors who are often the architects of strenuous and demanding standards to appoint others to the senior rank of *professor*. In some cases, the difficulties associated with earning the academic title of *professor* at some African universities are compounded by the Old School mentality of some pioneer professors not being willing to open up professorial doors to new and younger entrants in the academy. Instead, the Old School continue to devise different self-serving rules to protect and perpetuate the status quo in their favour. And the younger and dynamic academics have to wait until they too grow grey hairs before they can be considered for a professorial appointment.

That said, we are mindful also that, due to the harshness of the African economies, many academics in Africa hardly engage in active scholarly writing and have been reduced by economic hardship to serving merely as part-time petty traders, farmers, contractors, poultry organisers, pirate taxi operators, private tutors and so forth, just to make ends meet.[16] This unfortunate development keeps robbing many bright African academics of the opportunity to become Africa's coveted professors. As Mukwena observes, regarding parallel developments at a leading African university:

> Due to the economic crisis, some of the academics in privileged positions such as some Heads of Departments have at times disregarded professional considerations in their exploitation of certain work related survival opportunities such as seminars, workshops, conferences, research and consultancy. Some Heads of Departments...are known to nominate themselves to attend seminars and conferences abroad, even when such seminars and conferences are not exactly in the area of their specialisation and there are other colleagues who are well qualified and experienced in those areas. The over-riding consideration is usually how much money they will make from attending such conferences and seminars and not whether they are more suitable than others to attend the same.[17]

Mukwena continues:

> "Some academics who are well connected to donor agencies and international organisations have in some cases formed networks and hijacked a number of lucrative projects even those in which they are not well qualified

> and experienced to undertake, usually leaving out of such projects other academics who may be well qualified and experienced to undertake them."[18]

These are some of the politics surrounding academia in Africa, and such politics continue to shape the landscape for developing legal education in Africa today. There have been notorious cases, for example, especially in the natural sciences, the medical field and engineering sciences (involving research conducted in laboratory teams or project teams), where Heads of Departments (HOD) at some African universities are said to have issued instructions or given subtle hints to their subordinates that each and every research paper that will be published by any research or academic staff member in that department should carry the name of the HOD as the co-author. This would be the case even if the HOD did not contribute anything to the research paper. As a result, the position of HOD is seen by many academics as an attractive position because it not only guarantees the titleholder of higher perks and incentives, such as travelling to attend conferences, including earning some lucrative per diems, but it also assures the titleholder that he or she will be listed on every publication that will come out of the department. Consequently, it is often the case that when the HOD notices his name appearing on several publications, he can then nominate himself for a promotion and present his credentials before the university's promotions committee. Much of this is done based primarily on the so-called co-authored publications that the HOD was not even a part of.

Chapter 2

Primary University Qualifications to Become a Lawyer in the USA, the UK and South Africa

2.1 Creation of the Juris Doctor (JD) Degree in the US

In the US, for a student to graduate as a lawyer, the student normally has to complete seven years in university, taking both a pre-law Bachelors degree and three years of law school. This trend emulates developments in the medical profession where it takes a medical student approximately seven years to graduate from medical school and then obtain the title 'doctor'. This explains, in part, why, in the early 1960s, the US changed the title of the primary

American law degree from Bachelor of Laws degree (LLB) to Juris Doctor (JD) degree. As one report shows:

> The creation of the modern J.D. program is largely credited to Christopher Columbus Langdell, who served as dean of Harvard Law School from 1870 to 1895. Langdell dedicated his life to reforming legal education in the United States; the historian Robert Stevens wrote that 'it was Langdell's goal to turn the legal profession into a university educated one—and not at the undergraduate level, but through a three-year post baccalaureate degree.' He was generally successful in remaking most American law schools in Harvard's mold, since they often drew their faculty from Harvard. First, Harvard extended its LL.B. program from 18 months to two years in 1871, and then to three years in 1899. Then, in 1896, Harvard was the first law school to officially require an undergraduate degree as a prerequisite to admission (although the rule was not strictly enforced until 1909). By 1921, the same rule had been adopted by the law schools at Columbia, Pennsylvania, Case Western Reserve, Stanford, and Yale. Still, although the entry-level law program was revamped as a graduate program, the degree conferred continued to be called an LLB.[19]

The report continues:

> However, upon its opening in 1902, the University of Chicago chose to award the J.D. rather than the Bachelor of Laws. Some schools started conferring the J.D. as a Latin honor for students with high grades. Eventually, the disparate treatment prompted schools to abandon the distinction and call all degrees conferred a doctorate. Yale Law School was the last to rename the degree—it conferred the LL.B. until 1971.[20]

But, is a JD a true Doctorate? The polemics surrounding the switch from the LLB title to the JD have filled the pages of several

American journals and commentaries. It is, however, not the purpose of this book to revive such debates.

Suffice it to say, unlike the introduction of the title 'JD' in the US, UK law schools and those in other parts of the Commonwealth have retained the title 'Bachelor of Laws' degree for their primary law degree. Further, it normally takes three to four years of undergraduate study for a student to graduate as a lawyer in the UK and other parts of the Commonwealth. But, while the UK has retained the distinction between a barrister and a solicitor, many Commonwealth African States have now fused the roles of a barrister and a solicitor into one office. In these countries, the officeholder is usually referred to as an advocate.

2.2 Academic Developments in Canada, China, Australia and South Africa

Typically, while a law student in the US has to complete a Bachelors degree before he or she can be admitted to law school, this is not necessarily the case in the UK and other Commonwealth countries. As Richardson observes:

> As you are probably aware, the United States is composed of fifty states. Canada is composed of ten provinces and three territories. With the exception of the province of Quebec in Canada and the state of Louisiana in the US, the North American legal system is historically based on the system of common law that originated in England. This means that in many respects, law school curriculum in Canada and the US is similar to law school curriculum in the UK, Australia and New Zealand. In Canada and the US students normally enter law school after earning a bachelors degree. This is not so in the UK..., law school in the US is a three year academic programme which is undertaken after the completion of a bachelors degree.[21]

Although some universities in Canada, China and Australia, such as the University of Toronto,[22] the Chinese University of Hong Kong,[23] Bond University[24] and the University of Melbourne,[25] now offer the JD degree, this trend has not attracted much following in Commonwealth Africa. Even South Africa, which boasted of a graduate LLB degree programme, is now moving away from treating the primary law degree as a graduate qualification. Most universities in South Africa have introduced a four-year undergraduate LLB degree programme.[26] Prior to these changes, the South African system of legal education operated on a racially motivated three-tier system of qualifying lawyers. The LLB degree in South Africa was a graduate degree reserved mainly for the white South Africans, a few Asians and some coloured people. The other law degrees offered in South Africa, which are now abolished, were the Baccalaureus Procurationis degree (BProc) and the Bachelor of Jurisprudence (BJuris) degree. Unlike the LLB degree, these degrees were of inferior quality and were offered as undergraduate law degrees. The BProc and BJuris degrees were reserved mainly for black people. And law schools that had strong concentrations of the BProc and BJuris academic programs were meant to serve black people under the segregated system of apartheid education.[27] It also took less years and was less costly to obtain the BProc and BJuris degrees than it took and cost to complete the LLB.[28] This meant that, under the apartheid system, the majority of black people and other oppressed ethnic groups could only qualify for the BProc and BJuris degrees since most of the scholarships for postgraduate studies at LLB level went to the properly funded white universities. Yet the economically disenfranchised black students also needed a well-developed education system, with adequate funding, to enable them obtain the LLB degree.

While it was easy for most white South Africans to obtain government scholarships and bursaries to pursue LLB degree studies at white dominated universities, it was not easy for the disenfranchised blacks to gain access to such educational facilities at the black universities.[29] As Makosana observes,

> During the apartheid era, race was a primary factor that determined the funding of education in South Africa. The Bantu Education Act No. 47 of 1953 marshalled in state-mandated inequities in the funding of education. The implementation of this act racialized the provision of education in the country, resulting in poor funding of education for the Black population. In consequence, the burden of funding African/Black education was placed squarely on the shoulders of Black parents.[30]

And the paradox was that the LLB degree in South Africa was a prerequisite for one to gain admission to the Bar, as an advocate, and have the right of audience before the highest court of appeal in the land. Discrimination of this kind kept the whites in power. Towards the end of apartheid, it is alleged that some white people were getting desperate and eager to equip themselves and their fellow white South Africans with easily obtained academic qualifications so that when the blacks finally took over government, the whites would still have the best jobs in the country. Views have been expressed from different quarters that, in some cases, uncles would supervise PhD dissertations of nephews, while aunties and cousins would serve as external and internal examiners. But there is no doubt that South Africa has reasonably well developed institutions of higher learning. By contrast, what we are criticising here is not the institutions of learning *per se*, but the mentality and practice of those that were in authority under the apartheid educational system.

And, until recently, most South African universities denied many foreign African LLB graduates admission to the Master of Laws degree programmes (LLM) in South Africa. Yet, today, some of the top academicians in law schools of South Africa are foreign professionals from other African States. Most of these individuals obtained law degrees from their home country universities before pursuing graduate and postgraduate studies abroad. But how have these foreign professionals made it today in the same South Africa that used to deny foreign African LLB graduates admission to South African LLM programmes? Some of the arguments advanced against the admission of foreign African LLB graduates were that the South African LLB, like the American JD, was a graduate degree and, further, that South Africa followed the Roman-Dutch law system unlike many other African countries.

Although many LLM degree programmes in South Africa somewhat mirror the structure of other LLMs in the Commonwealth—that is, as a self-sustaining degree programme that is independent of the LLB curriculum—and not the typical American LLM which is usually a sandwich programme of the JD curriculum, many South African universities treated LLB degrees from other African universities with suspect. Yet, American law schools, for example, though having a graduate JD programme, like South Africa, did not discriminate against LLB graduates from credible African law schools. Neither did the UK law schools have difficulties in admitting African students to their LLM and PhD programmes. Nevertheless, the demise of apartheid in South Africa has now ended this indecent intellectual circus.

2.3 The American JD Degree

In the US, the JD degree is a first professional degree in law offered at graduate level.[31] By contrast, the LLB degree in the UK and other Commonwealth States, as already pointed out, is a first professional degree in law offered at undergraduate level. That said, the American JD degree is neither a Masters degree nor a Doctorate degree. Commenting on the standard of the JD degree, Pappas observes:

> The JD is not a doctorate degree. In fact, the next degree after the JD in the US is the LLM and then the doctorate degree (SJD), which is offered by some law schools. The JD and LLB essentially contain the same exact standard and level of courses, such as torts, criminal, evidence, land law (real estate). In fact, how ironic that most JD graduates from US ABA law schools have never taken Jurisprudence as part of the work! To equate a doctorate degree with the number of years spent in one's educational system has no bearing whatsoever on the whether the degree is really a doctorate degree. Quality and standard of course work required is the benchmark, not the number of years spent in an educational system. The US JD was in fact an LLB prior to 1960. In fact, past LLB holders were contacted by many law schools to convert their LLB into JD's. That is not a doctorate degree. I will concede this point however, to the extent that the JD is taken in the US after four years of college or university work, it is a 'postgraduate degree.' That is not the same thing as being a doctorate degree in law. That is a separate degree offered after completion of the JD and the LLM. The JD is only a doctorate degree in name only. Form is the not the same thing as substance.[32]

Contributing to the same debate, Cromwell adds:

> The JD was part of the inflation of degrees by designation whereby the traditional postgraduate seminary degree was the Bachelor of Divinity which became labelled as a Master of Divinity. The notion of a law degree as necessarily a postgraduate degree is a comparatively recent development. As late as the 1920s there were continuing debates within state bar associations as to whether it was necessary for lawyers to have any undergraduate college background. Now most states require two years, which, in my judgment is somewhat absurd. It does not matter if most law schools require two or three years college, or that most law students have a four-year undergraduate degree; any one who can pass the bar, law school,

> undergraduate degree or no degree, two years college or no years college, on-line law school training, correspondence law school training, University of London external training (which is an EXCELLENT means of a very sound law degree which reasonably should meet the basic requirements for entry level exams in the US, and should be so recognized by State bars). Traditionally, high school was all that was required for the formal study of law (that most students were college graduates is irrelevant).[33]

Adding further, Cromwell goes on to say:

> In the 1930s many high school clerical workers in Washington attended the National Law College and obtained the LLB or even the graduate degree, LLM. Later the National Law College was absorbed into George Washington University School of Law, and later the degrees, the LLB degrees, were changed to a JD from George Washington University, thus making high school graduates who attended National Law College JD graduates of an ABA approved law school. I think euphemism, symbolism, and charade were the primary factors in attempting to elevate the title of the first degree in law. As a distinct field, LLB is apt and appropriate as a first processional degree, the JD is the equivalent, and, in my judgment, has nothing to do with any recognition of being some sort of graduate type degree. It definitely is not, even though many people with a JD have a BSc in something, and most schools demand it.[34]

Against this background, we now turn to examine the academic standing of a JD degree.

2.4 The Academic Rank of a JD

In the US and elsewhere, a number of theories and assertions, surrounding the pecking order at which a JD should be placed, have preceded and followed through from the time the JD was introduced.

Is a JD equivalent to a Doctorate? Let us, first, take a more reasoned look at the origins of the title 'Doctor'.

> The term 'doctor', meaning teacher or instructor, originated with the ancient Romans for those who lectured publicly on philosophical topics. During the Middle Ages, it was used as a title of honour for men of great learning. It was first made an academic title at the University of Bologna which was allowed by the emperor to appoint doctores legum (doctors of laws). The University of Paris followed suit in the year 1145. Soon after, popes granted the universities the right to appoint doctors canonum et decretalium (teachers of the canon law) and when the study of civil law was combined with that of the canon law, the title was changed to doctor utriusque juris (teacher of both laws). The faculties of theology and medicine followed that of law in conferring this title. The doctorate is given beyond the baccalaureate degree and requires several years of advanced study, the successful completion of a thesis or dissertation, and written and oral examinations.[35]

Yet, the American Bar Association (ABA), in a self-serving and egocentric statement to try and inflate the image of the JD degree, given that the JD is the main and principal qualification for an individual to practice or teach law in the US,[36] argues that the JD is equivalent to a PhD degree.[37] In a seemingly desperate statement, ABA postulates as follows:

> *2. J.D. Degree – Ph.D. Degree Equivalency*
>
> WHEREAS, the acquisition of a Doctor of Jurisprudence (J.D.) degree requires from 84 to 90 semester hours of post baccalaureate study and the Doctor of Philosophy (Ph.D.) degree usually requires 60 semester hours of post baccalaureate study along with the writing of a dissertation, the two degrees shall be considered as equivalent degrees for educational employment purposes;

> THEREFORE, BE IT RESOLVED, that all appropriate persons be requested to eliminate any policy, or practice, existing within their jurisdiction which disparages legal education or promotes discriminatory employment practices against J.D. degree-holders who hold academic appointment in education institutions.[38]

The position taken by ABA, regarding the standing of an ABA accredited JD degree and how such a degree compares with a PhD, raises illogical difficulties. ABA's argument focuses quite narrowly on the number of academic credits allocated to the JD and to the taught component of most PhD programmes at universities in the US, without really broadening out to include the weighting of the research and dissertation component of the PhD.

Besides, the argument advanced by some proponents of the 'JD is equivalent to PhD' theory, arguing that, generally, JD students serve as law review editors while they are in law school, does not resolve the conundrum here. For the most part, JD students are not involved in the writing of major publications or lengthy dissertations other than writing a few short papers for certain courses on the JD programme and editing some article submissions from law professors for the law reviews. And not every JD student will serve on the editorial board of a law review. Admission to serve on such boards is often competitive. So, the argument that JD students serve on editorial boards of law reviews, in addition to writing several term papers, does not hold water here.

Unlike ABA's unfortunate statement, regarding its view of the JD degree as the equivalent of a PhD, the U.S. Department of Education, a federal governmental body, distinguishes between first-professional degrees and research Doctorates.[39] According to the U.S. Department of Education,

> It is also important to recognize that first-professional degrees...are first degrees, not graduate research degrees.

> Several of the degree titles in this group of subjects…incorporate the term 'Doctor,' but they are not research doctorates and not equivalent to the Ph.D. Master's degrees and research doctorates in these fields of study are awarded, but they have different names and students enroll in those programs after having earned a first-professional degree.[40]

And we have already seen above that, in contrast to the views advanced by ABA, many commentators, including the US Department of Education, hold the view that a JD degree cannot be said to be, and is not, equivalent to a PhD degree. The JD is, therefore, not a 'true Doctorate'. Indeed, this position fits in well with the argument that a true Doctorate represents the most advanced degree conferred by an institution of higher learning. By all comparison, a JD does not constitute such a degree.

As Harvard University Law School points out, regarding its Doctor of Juridical Science degree (SJD), the SJD, modelled on the very best PhD programmes in other disciplines,[41] is Harvard Law School's most advanced law degree, designed for aspiring legal academics who wish to pursue sustained independent study, research and writing.[42] Also, the University of Virginia Law School explains the JD even better by stating that 'the Juris Doctor is the basic degree required for entrance into the legal profession.'[43] By contrast, 'to earn the Doctor of Juridical Science (SJD), the Law School's most advanced research degree,' the University of Virginia adds that 'students must demonstrate superior intellectual ability in a programme approved by the graduate committee.'[44]

Similarly, Pace University Law School points out that, 'as the most advanced degree in the law, SJD programmes are authorised at only 22 of the 176 law schools accredited by the American Bar Association (ABA) in the US and Pace has one of only a few SJD programmes specialising in environmental law.'[45] Further, the International Center for Legal Studies observes that, in the US, as with the rest of the world, 'the advanced law degree above the JD continues to be the LLM or Master of Laws and the degree above that is the SJD, JSD or LLD—the true 'Doctor of Laws' degree.'[46]

Yet, to the contrary, there are publicists who argue in favour of two types of Doctorates: a professional Doctorate and an academic Doctorate. To illustrate, a report by the University of Ioannina School of Medicine provides as follows:

> The doctor's degree represents the most advanced earned degree conferred by most institutions. There are two distinct types: the practitioner's degree and the research degree. The first type represents advanced training for the practice of various professions, principally Doctor of Medicine, Juris Doctor and Doctor of Dental Surgery. These degrees carry no implication of original research. The second type is a research doctorate representing prolonged periods of advanced study. A dissertation which usually accompanies the study is intended to contribute substantially to existing knowledge on the subject. The most important of these, the Doctor of Philosophy, no longer has an implication of philosophy for its holder, but represents advanced research in any of the major fields of knowledge. It was first awarded in the United States in 1861 by Yale University. Its counterpart, the Doctor of Science, reflects the successful completion of work and a dissertation beyond the practitioner's degree.[47]

A JD, some argue,[48] like a medical doctor's qualification, the MD, is a professional Doctorate, while a PhD is an academic Doctorate. Proponents of this theory tend to place the JD degree in the same category of professional Doctorates such as the Doctor of Business Administration degree (DBA), the Doctor of Engineering degree (DEng), the Doctor of Architecture degree (DArch), the Doctor of Creative Arts degree (DCA), the Doctor of Environmental Design degree (DED), the Doctor of Health Psychology degree (DHPsych), the Doctor of Health Services Management degree (DHSM), the Doctor of Public Administration degree (DPA), the Doctor of Public Health degree (DPH), the Doctor of Psychology degree (DPsych) and the Doctor of Nursing degree (DNurs). Convincing as this argument may seem, it is somewhat misleading. The DBA, DEng, DArch, DPA degrees, plus many other professional Doctorates, stand above a Masters degree and are seen by many as being almost at par with a PhD.

2.5 Is a JD Degree a Professional Doctorate in the Real Sense?

Normally, a candidate for a professional Doctorate will have obtained not only a Bachelors degree in the concerned field, but a Masters degree as well in addition to some relevant practical experience.[49] Besides, most professional Doctorates, unlike a JD, have both taught and research components, culminating in the preparation and presentation of a major thesis or dissertation.[50] As Queensland University of Technology points out:

> A professional doctorate is defined by the Australian Council of Deans and Directors of Graduate Studies as: "*a program of research and advanced study which enables the candidate to make a significant contribution to knowledge and practice in their professional context. In so doing, the candidate may also contribute more generally to scholarship within a discipline or field of study.*"[51]

However, Pillips and Pugh, writing from a UK perspective, counter-argue against the idea of equating a professional Doctorate with a PhD:

> The point of a doctorate is that it recognizes an independent contribution to the subject rather than taught work, however advanced. Education, clinical psychology and business administration are fields where degrees of EdD, DClincPsy, and DBA are being considered at present. The argument is that if medical practitioners obtain the title of doctor, so should advanced practitioners in these and other fields. In our view the acceptance of these degrees would be a considerable dilution in the concept of the doctorate. This is a recognition that the successful candidate has carried out independent research to a high level. Practitioner qualifications should remain linked to the master's-level qualification.[52]

It is important to observe that the title of 'doctor', as it applies to medical practitioners today, has evolved over many years and generations. It has not been a product of academic politics and semantics. To elaborate, one view states that since medical practitioners spend approximately seven years in university before obtaining their Doctor of Medicine degree (MD)—all things be equal, that is the approximate time it would take to obtain a Bachelors degree, a Masters degree and a PhD sequentially—like PhD holders, medical practitioners should be honoured with the title of 'doctor'. If, on the other hand, this is the basis upon which proponents in support of the title of 'doctor' for JDs would like to proceed, then the argument takes a different twist. Indeed, the reasons that could have favoured the approval and recognition of MDs for the title of 'doctor' may not be applicable to JDs today. As Phillips and Pugh argue:

> In medicine, the practice is even stranger: general medical practitioners are given the honorary title of Doctor although they do not have a doctorate from their universities. Indeed, on the basis of their university course they are credited with two bachelor's degrees, although having a licence to practice they exemplify the concept of

> a master's degree. There are, of course, good historical reasons for these anomalies. The concept of a university doctorate has always been clear. As the highest degree that can be awarded, it proclaims that the recipient is worthy of being listened to *as an equal* by the appropriate university faculty.[53]

2.6 How is the JD Degree Viewed by the Legal Community Outside America?

In many Commonwealth countries that have not succumbed to pressures of the American JD culture, a JD is treated, for all intents and purposes, as the equivalent of an undergraduate LLB degree. This is so because the JD and LLB are both first-professional degrees. We submit that the time spent studying for a pre-JD degree should not count as part of law school time since a pre-JD degree is usually taken in a discipline that is outside law school. So, law school alone, when pursuing the American JD degree, is three years only. And this is exactly the same amount of time and coursework it takes and involves to complete law school at most universities in Commonwealth countries.

In spite of the fact that the American JD is a graduate degree and that the LLB degree at many universities in other common law systems is, generally speaking, an undergraduate degree, that view alone does not change an iota of the substance and content of the JD and LLB degrees. An instructive note from Oxford University, regarding the study of law at Oxford, follows hereunder:

> Among legal practitioners and legal academics alike, Oxford's *Bachelor of Civil Law* (BCL) degree is the most highly esteemed masters-level qualification in the common law world. The BCL standard is higher than that required in a first law degree, such as a BA, LLB, or JD. This is reflected in more demanding classes, harder

> work, and tougher examination standards. Courses are not introductory and those who choose subjects in which they have no background at all should expect to invest heavily in independent preparation.[54]

Confirming Oxford's view that a JD is a basic law degree equivalent to the LLB, even the University of Columbia Law School, which is one of America's best law schools, admits that a JD is, indeed, a basic law degree, and that graduate studies at the University of Columbia Law School are 'designed for students who… earned *a basic law degree (the U.S. Juris Doctor [J.D.] degree or its foreign equivalent*).'[55] Yet, there are those that still argue superficially not only for the superiority of the American JD over the LLB in other common law jurisdictions, but also that JD graduates are entitled to use the title 'Doctor' before their name.[56] However, as one commentator observes:

> 'Doctor' *Lawyer*?: Legal terminology, with its liberal use of Latin phrases and other specialized jargon, can be daunting and confusing. More annoying…is the practice of some attorneys using the title 'Doctor.' Although there is apparently some dispute over this, I view it as misleading, cheesy, unseemly, and self-embarrassing for a lawyer (with a JD, that is) to refer to himself as 'Doctor' such-and-such. In addition, the law degree is usually a Juris Doctor (JD), yet many lawyers insist on calling it a 'Juris Doctorate', I suppose out of ignorance or to make it sound more impressive. (Note: a few law schools apparently do use 'Juris Doctorate' on their diplomas—improperly, in my view.) Way back then, lawyers got an LLB (the bachelor of laws—the 'LL' meaning, I suppose, 'laws'-plural in much the same way that §§ means 'sections'). A master's in law is an LLM, and a true doctorate in law is an LLD (also sometimes given as a straight PhD, or as an SJD or JSD—for 'doctor of juridical/juristic science').[57]

The same commentator goes on to provide further insights, highlighting the following:

> Apparently, a few decades ago, the American legal bar decided to change the LLB to the JD, in a vain attempt to garner the prestige of PhDs or MDs. Under today's rules, one must obtain a bachelor's degree in *anything*, before entering law school. This does make the 3-year law degree technically a graduate degree, but since the undergrad degree need not relate in the slightest to law (my own undergraduate degree is in engineering!), it is not really a graduate degree in the sense of building on some foundation, and it is thus absurd to view the law degree as a true doctorate. Query: if a regular JD lawyer is a 'Doctor,' what does he become after subsequently obtaining an LLD?—a Doctor-Doctor? Many non-American lawyers, incidentally, still obtain LLB degrees, though some seem to be following the American model to change from LLB to JD (without requiring an undergraduate degree though!). This may all be academic (I am not sure if the pun is intended), as the prestige behind the PhD degree and the 'doctor' title continue to plummet, due to lowering of standards and the explosion of PhDs granted in ridiculous specialties.[58]

Hitherto, law schools in Commonwealth Africa have not been affected by the politics of the American JD degree. Whereas a number of Australian and Canadian law schools, including some Asian law schools, are increasingly succumbing to pressures of Americanizing their primary legal education, Commonwealth African law schools have remained markedly unshaken. The LLB degree, as an undergraduate qualification,[59] is still the principal university degree for an individual to qualify as a lawyer in Commonwealth Africa.[60] In countries such as Ghana,[61] Zambia[62] and South Africa,[63] some law schools are increasingly attracting candidates who already have an academic degree in another discipline to pursue the LLB degree. Even so, the status of the graduate LLB degree has not been elevated above the status of the undergraduate LLB degree in a manner that ABA tries to glorify the American JD degree. And neither do universities in Commonwealth Africa nor elsewhere (including some well-regarded law schools in India, such as the National Law School of India,[64] offering the integrated five-year programme that culminates in joint 'BA, LLB degrees' at undergraduate level) consider a graduate LLB as the equivalent of a PhD. The LLB degree, whether offered at undergraduate or graduate level, like its American counterpart, the JD degree, is, for all intents and purposes, a first-professional degree in law.

It could be argued, however, that the only major advantage that a holder of a JD degree would have over the holder of an LLB degree is that the JD curriculum, together with the pre-JD Bachelors degree, equips US law graduates with inter-disciplinary and multi-disciplinary skills that are much deeper rooted than those found on many Commonwealth LLB programmes. Furthermore, in a country such as the US, where there is a law school in each and every corner of almost every major city, having a JD as a graduate degree helps to put a lid on the ever increasing numbers of lawyers. Indeed, if law degrees in the US were to be offered as undergraduate degrees, there would be an explosion in numbers of lawyers, especially that the US public is, generally speaking, more litigious than many other publics. Everyone in the US would try to become a lawyer and capitalise financially on the highly litigious US public. However, the length of time it takes to become a lawyer in the US is well suited for that country. The seven-year period is good enough to discourage others from getting into law school and thereby avoid an influx of lawyers on the market.

By contrast, the economic argument 'to discourage others from getting into law school' does not have much attraction in smaller economies, such as those in Commonwealth Africa, that do not have several competing law schools. For example, Zambia, Swaziland, Botswana and Namibia have only one law school each—that is, the University of Zambia, the University of Swaziland, the University of Botswana and the University of Namibia, respectively. There is need for these countries to train more lawyers as they struggle to build strong institutions and structures to support a sustainable culture of democracy and the rule of law. Indeed, the idea of introducing a mandatory post-Bachelors law degree, such as the American JD, to replace the undergraduate LLB, would be ill advised for a number of small economies in Commonwealth Africa. Besides, what qualities, aside from the deep-seated interdisciplinary and multidisciplinary qualities, can a JD offer which an LLB cannot offer? And it is not entirely correct to argue that law schools will get much more intellectual rigour and depth from graduate students who have obtained their Bachelors degrees in fields outside legal education before entering law school than from undergraduate students who come straight from high school. Oxford University, for example, like Cambridge University and many other top universities in the Commonwealth, offers a first-professional degree in law at undergraduate,[65] yet Oxford has produced some of the finest and most brilliant legal minds in legal practice and academia today.

Chapter 3

Post-JD Qualifications and the Issue of their Recognition

3.1 Introduction

In the US, many lawyers consider the JD degree not only as the appropriate qualification to gain admission to the Bar, but also as the ideal qualification to enter the world of academia.[66] In short, genuine legal education in the US starts and ends with the JD. Anything else purporting to exist beyond or ahead of the JD is seen by many in the US as merely speculative and less worthy pursuing. The American Bar Association (ABA) points out:

> Standard 308 of the ABA Standards for Approval of Law Schools states that an ABA-approved law school may not establish a degree program in addition to its J.D. degree program unless the school is fully approved, and the additional degree program will not detract from a law school's ability to maintain a sound J.D. degree program.[67]

As noted below, apart from the approval of the first professional degree in law, the JD, ABA does not approve of any other law degree program at any ABA accredited law school.[68] According to ABA,

> ABA accreditation does not extend to any program supporting any other degree granted by the law school. Rather the content and requirements of those degrees, such as an LL.M., are created by the law school itself and do not reflect any judgment by the ABA accrediting bodies regarding the quality of the program. Moreover, admission requirements for such programs, particularly with regard to foreign students, vary from school to school, and are not evaluated through the ABA accreditation process. The ABA reviews post-JD degree programs only to determine whether the offering of such post-JD program would have an adverse impact on the law school's ability to maintain its accreditation for the JD program. If no adverse impact is indicated, the ABA 'acquiesces' in the law school's decision to offer the non-JD program and degree.[69]

And ABA has adopted a statement that no post-JD degree or other graduate program is a substitute for the JD and should not be considered the equivalent of the JD for bar admission purposes.[70] Clearly, the legal profession in the US has remained insular, closed out from the rest of world outside the US. ABA's statement here that 'no post-JD degree or other graduate program is a substitute for the JD and should not be considered the equivalent of the JD for bar admission purposes' entails that foreign lawyers without an American JD degree, but with credible law degrees—even where the primary law degree was obtained from a strong common law jurisdiction such as the UK—have to struggle in the US to gain professional recognition or to make it into law practice or academia. Yet, the American legal system is based on the common law system. Some critics may, however, argue that there is a fundamental difference between the English common law and America's own version of the common law. But, for all intents and purposes, a recognizable law degree from a decent university in a common law jurisdiction should be able to equip the degree holder with transferable skills to adapt quickly to a foreign common law system. However, the US legal system is largely blind to such views. Similarly, in South Africa, such anomalies were seen when, prior to the end of apartheid, credible law degrees from other African countries outside South Africa, except those from the then racist Zimbabwe, were denied ample recognition. Until the end of apartheid, South Africa remained an insular and xenophobic environment in as far as development of legal education was concerned.

A fear is expressed here that if, in the US, the development of legal education, together with the need for the US to recognize credible and decent foreign law degrees from common law jurisdictions, for purposes of permitting foreign trained lawyers to enter legal practice or academia, does not quickly respond to and embrace the concept of globalization and how the world is increasingly becoming a network of international economic relations, the US legal profession will forever remain insular and xenophobic. And the American JD will only command a higher status than the LLB within the US alone, including in a few foreign jurisdictions, such as Canada and Australia, where the notion of the superiority of the American JD over the LLB seems to have earned some modest sympathy.

3.2 JD as the Primary Qualification to Practice Law and Enter Academia in the US

In the US, post-JD degrees such as the Master of Laws (LLM) degree and the Doctor of Juridical Science (SJD or JSD) degree have limited credibility in as far as the value of a degree is concerned in the pursuit of a professional career in law practice or academia. As the University of Columbia Law School points out:

> International lawyers who intend to reside permanently and to practice law in the United States should apply for the J.D. degree, the first degree in law, rather than the LL.M. The J.D. program is normally three years of full-time study. Generally, a maximum of one year's advanced standing toward the J.D. degree at Columbia may be granted for graduate legal studies completed in the United States or another common law country. Such standing, however, is determined on an individual basis by request of the student after an offer of admission has been made. No advanced standing is given for legal studies completed in a civil law country. Completion of an LL.M. degree at Columbia Law School does not guarantee admission to the J.D. program. Law firms have proved generally reluctant to offer permanent employment to foreign-trained lawyers.[71]

In the US, the common practice for JD graduates who intend to enter academia is for them to clerk for a notable judge or serve as an Associate at a prestigious law firm before they can be considered for appointment as a faculty member at some reputable law school.[72] Seldom do American trained lawyers go on to pursue a post-JD qualification, such as an LLM degree or an SJD degree even if they intend to join academia.

Another route for a career in academia, though less traversed than the one outlined above, is for a JD graduate to pursue a teaching fellowship at a leading US law school.[73] There are several such law teaching fellowships and they include the Reginald F. Lewis Fellowship for Law Teaching at Harvard Law School, the William Hastie Fellowship Program at the University of Wisconsin Law School, the Charles Hamilton Houston Fellowship for Law Teaching at Harvard Law School, the Graduate Fellowship Program for Future Law Professors at Georgetown University Law Center, the Robert M. Cover Fellowships in Clinical Teaching at Yale Law School, the Harry A. Bigelow Teaching Fellowships at the University of Chicago Law

School, the Associates in Law Program at Columbia University Law School, the John M. Olin Fellows and Scholars in Law and Economics at the University of Chicago Law School, the Teaching Fellowship Program at Stanford Law School, the Faculty Fellows Program at the University of Iowa College of Law, and the Graduate Teaching Fellowship Program at Temple University School of Law.[74]

However, most US law teaching fellowships hardly go to foreigners who are prospective law professors.[75] As noted above, the system is quite insular and, in the majority of cases, it only admits US candidates who are already JD graduates from ABA accredited law schools.[76] As Georgetown University Law Center points out, regarding its Graduate Fellowship Program for Future Law Professors,

> Law teaching has always been one of the most challenging and highly sought after careers in the legal profession. The traditional routes for entry into law teaching have been available only to a select number of graduates. In 1989 Georgetown University Law Center created a graduate fellowship to expand the avenues available to talented law school graduates who aspire to become law professors. We hope to attract candidates who can bring a variety of perspectives to the development of legal scholarship and increase the diversity of the law teaching profession. *Foreign-trained lawyers are not eligible to apply to the Future Law Professors Program... Applicants must hold a JD degree from an ABA accredited law school.*[77]

On a similar note, Stanford Law School has the following policy, regarding admission to its Law Teaching Fellowship Programme:

> Stanford Law School invites applications for Legal Research and Writing Instructors/Lecturers in law for the forthcoming academic year (2007-08)... *Qualifications*: J.D. and at least 2 years of clerkship or law practice experience before the start of the term of employment.[78]

And the University of California at Los Angeles Law School sets out the following statement, regarding admission to its Law Teaching Fellowship Programme:

> The Fellowship program lasts one or two years, during which time the Fellow will: complete a substantial scholarly publication and present the publication as a work-in-progress to the UCLA School of Law Faculty; teach courses in two out of four semesters of the fellowship; assist with other Williams Institute research, publications, and events; permit the Institute to publish any article(s) resulting from the Fellowship – as long as such publication will not interfere with the Fellow's ability to publish such articles in the law journal; acknowledge the Institute's assistance in any published work that is facilitated by the Fellowship; and work closely with the faculty mentor in order to observe and participate in teaching, as well as to complete a publishable scholarly piece. *Qualifications*: Candidates must hold a JD from an ABA accredited law school and be committed to a career of law teaching and scholarship…[79]

That said, on the Associates-in-Law Programme at Columbia University Law School some Australian, British and Canadian trained lawyers have managed to gain admission.[80] But it is doubtful if the same can be said of many African lawyers aspiring to become academics.

In general, there are three well-trodden paths to a career in law teaching in the US, and a great majority of law teachers—though not all—entered law teaching by one of these paths.[81] According to Leiter, the following are the three main paths:[82]

> *Path A:* The Classical Path starts with an exceptional academic performance in law school (e.g., ranking in the top 5% of one's class), service on the law review, preferably in a senior editorial position (e.g., 'Articles Editor,' 'Editor-in-Chief,' etc.), followed by a prestigious judicial clerkship, at least on a U.S. Court of Appeals and, if possible, on the U.S. Supreme Court…

> *Path B:* The Modified Classical Path is a somewhat less demanding approximation of the Classical Path: e.g., a strong academic performance, but perhaps not exceptional; some work on a journal, or some substantial writing experience, but perhaps not via law review; some practical experience, either in practice or some sort of clerkship, if not a U.S. Court of Appeals... The *key* to the Modified Classical Path is usually the pursuit of a graduate law degree (an LL.M. or S.J.D.) at a law school that is conventionally regarded as more prestigious... Of course, the degree is really just a proxy for the real key, which is to complete some publishable scholarly work while pursuing the degree, and at the same time suitably impress the faculty at the LLM/SJD school...
>
> *Path C:* The Interdisciplinary Path is often combined with Paths A and B, though it need not be if the work in the other discipline is of sufficient quality and distinction to attract the attention of law schools. Here the candidate also pursues graduate studies in another area of relevance to law – e.g., history, economics, philosophy, sociology, political science – earning at least an M.A. or, better, a Ph.D... One important caveat about these three paths to law teaching. Most law schools are, more than anything else, looking for potential *scholars*.[83]

By comparison, although a number of UK law schools have in the past recruited academics who hold only a first degree in law—that is, the LLB degree, as long as such candidates can demonstrate potential or evidence of strong scholarship—this trend is slowly coming to an end. The practice now favours the recruitment of individuals who have, in addition to the LLB or JD degree, a postgraduate research degree such as a PhD. In fact, some universities in the UK insist that for a member of the academic staff to supervise a PhD student, that particular staff member should hold a PhD. The idea behind this rule is that the supervisor himself must be aware of the various issues surrounding the preparation, writing, supervision and examination of a PhD thesis.

The American SJD degree, by contrast, does not attract the same kind of attention as a PhD in law from a strong common law jurisdiction outside the US. In fact, most SJD and LLM programmes in the US, unlike programmes for the ABA accredited JD, attract limited funding from both within and outside the university. As such, academic standards on the LLM and SJD programmes are often compromised. Indeed, many post-JD programmes receive poor funding. And, in a way, as many legal scholars in Africa argue, the American SJD, for example, does not command the same academic respect that a British PhD commands. This point helps to explain why some foreign-trained lawyers who decide to enter academia in the US, after obtaining an American LLM or SJD degree, are often confined to teaching Third World oriented courses such as a few non-JD offerings that are part of the LLM curricula at many US law schools. Given that these individuals do not possess a US law degree that is accredited by ABA, they are seen in many circles as lacking the necessary skills and knowledge to impart on the core courses of the accredited JD programme. They are left to teach and supervise research on LLM and SJD programmes that are filled with foreign students and are not even accredited by ABA.

3.3 What to do with the Post-JD Degrees from America

In the US, there is a general perception among lawyers that if a person decides to pursue a post-JD law qualification, such as an LLM or SJD, then his or her JD was ‘not good enough’. Here, the term ‘not good enough’ entails that, at graduation, the JD was ranked in the lower echelon of academic performance or the JD was obtained from a lowly ranked law school. Often, individuals who feel insecure about their JD ‘not being good enough’ tend to register for an LLM degree at a highly ranked law school—preferably at an Ivy League law school—so as to catch up on the missed opportunity on the JD. That said, there are some JD graduates who are genuinely interested in pursuing post-JD qualifications, in spite of having graduated with high honours on the JD. Most of these graduates tend to pursue PhDs in fields related to law or in a field related to their pre-law school qualification.

We have already seen above that the two major post-JD academic programmes in the US are the LLM and the SJD degrees. However, some American universities have different titles for their post-JD qualifications, referring to the SJD, for example, as JSD. Others have slight variations of the post-JD qualifications, such as the Master of Civil Law (MCL) degree and the Doctor of Comparative Law (DCL) degree. And all these post-JD qualifications do not carry the same amount of professional prestige as the JD qualification. In fact, the majority of students that enrol on the LLM and SJD programmes are foreigners. As one report shows,

> In the USA, the LLM is a degree taken almost exclusively by foreign students. These students undertake subjects from the curriculum of the Juris Doctor (JD) degree, the basic law degree comparable with the Australian LLB.[84]

There are many reasons why foreign-trained lawyers go for the post-JD degree qualifications in the US. First, a number of foreign-trained lawyers, in pursuit of the American dream of migrating and working in the US, realise that they have already qualified in their home country as professional lawyers. With this in mind, they feel that there is no point in repeating a basic law degree, pegged at the LLB level, and that they should instead proceed directly to graduate studies and obtain an LLM degree or an SJD degree. Their hope is to increase chances of gaining employment. But little do foreign-trained lawyers realise that in many US universities the LLM is a degree designed and reserved for foreign students. The curriculum of the LLM degree in the majority of US universities is composed of a few courses carved out of the JD curriculum. It therefore makes no sense for an American-trained lawyer, holding a good JD degree, to pursue an LLM degree in the US.

For a number of foreign-trained lawyers, nomenclature misleads them and reality only dawns when they are admitted to the LLM degree programme. These foreign-trained lawyers find that they are taking subjects from the curriculum of the JD for their LLM. The feeling for many of them is like getting back to undergraduate and studying the basic courses on the LLB degree programme. By contrast, most LLM degree programmes in the UK, and elsewhere in the Commonwealth, are not extracted from the LLB curriculum. These degrees are independent and self-sustaining postgraduate qualifications. The LLM degree programmes at some universities in Commonwealth countries expose students to the nexus between law and related social science disciplines. In other cases, the LLM degree programme provides students with the opportunity to master a specialised field of law. In contrast, for the American LLM programme, it is difficult to appreciate how an individual can master a subject by choosing a cocktail of courses from the JD menu and just adding one or two extra courses from outside the JD curriculum.

Further, in the US, one other reason why foreign-trained lawyers go for the post-JD qualifications is that the cost of tuition and university fees on the JD programme are quite prohibitive. It is cheaper for a foreign-trained lawyer to pursue a nine-month LLM degree programme, say, at Harvard or Columbia, and then quickly proclaim that he or she is actually a graduate of Harvard Law School or Columbia University Law School, as the case may be. Often a time, such individuals tend to mute out information, intentionally and purposely, on where they obtained their primary law degree, mentioning only that they are graduates of some prestigious Ivy League law school.

Where a foreign-trained lawyer is considering an academic career in the US or outside the US, the idea of pursuing both the American LLM and SJD degrees may seem attractive since the names of those degrees appear to be the closest in nomenclature to the names of degrees awarded by universities in the Commonwealth (in particular the LLM and PhD in law degrees from Commonwealth countries). Other reasons why foreign-trained lawyers choose to undertake the American LLM and SJD degrees include a desire to be exposed to the legal system of the US. Some foreign-trained lawyers go for the American LLM and SJD degrees because of a desire to study subjects that can later form the basis of professional accreditation and Bar admission in the US.

There are also other foreign-trained lawyers who wish to undertake an LLM in the US but do not want to engage in the more specialised studies typical of advanced coursework LLM programmes in Commonwealth countries. These students are attracted to the core law subjects taught on the JD programme, such as Tort, Equity, Property and Contract. But overall, a number of American law schools are constructing these post-JD degrees, which Americans themselves shun and do not even attach much value to, as a way of making easy money out of desperate foreign-trained lawyers who either want to break into the US job market or have limited knowledge and information on the US system of legal education and law practice. However, critics of this view could argue that American law schools are simply responding to dictates of the market economy and, thus, constructing post-JD programmes that encourage and accommodate foreign-trained lawyers to construct their LLM curriculum from the regular course offerings of the JD programme. Interesting and innovative as this view may seem, systems that encourage the building of 'sandwich' *postgraduate* degree programmes from the curriculum of a *first-professional degree*, such as a JD, should be viewed with suspicion and caution.

The polemics surrounding the American LLM and SJD degrees, and why African students who go abroad to study law—whether pursuing a first-professional degree in law, a Masters or a Doctorate—ought to be careful with the type of law degrees they choose are well expressed by a Nigerian commentator who states:

> If you go to school and someone tries to give you a degree that your professor does not have, JUST SAY NO! If your professor has JD, then get JD. If he has Ph.D., get Ph.D. Do not go there and start getting something like Xh.D., PJD, SJD, etc.[85]

3.4 Disparities in Academic Standards on American LLM and SJD Programmes

An additional reason why the American LLM and SJD programmes attract mainly foreign students is that the admission requirements for both the LLM and SJD, particularly with regard to foreign students, vary from school to school, and are not evaluated through the ABA accreditation process.[86] And as further proof of the disparities in standards of post-JD qualifications, some US law schools require that a prospective SJD applicant completes an LLM at that very university where he or she intends to pursue the SJD, irrespective of whether or not he or she already has an LLM from another top rated American law school.[87] To illustrate, the University of Yale Law School has the following admission policy:

> The Doctor of the Science of Law (JSD) program is open only to LLM graduates of the Yale Law School. Students who have earned an LLM degree from another institution are admitted rarely and only under extraordinary circumstances.[88]

Similarly, the University of Pennsylvania Law School insists that applications and admissions to its SJD programme normally are open to those who have spent at least one academic year as a resident student at Penn Law School, typically an applicant who earned the LLM degree from Penn Law School.[89] In exceptional circumstances, this requirement may be waived, but only if the applicant has earned a graduate law degree equivalent to the LLM from another law school and has already published a substantial body of legal scholarship in English.[90] By contrast, such dogmatic rigidities are, largely speaking, uncharacteristic of universities in the Commonwealth.

3.5 The Credibility of American LLM and SJD Degrees

Chief Justice Randall T. Shepard of the US observed in his 1999 letter to all the state Chief Justices, liaison judges, and Directors of Boards of Bar Examiners, clarifying ABA's role in post-JD programmes:

> I am writing you at the request of the Council of the Section of Legal Education and Admissions to the Bar of the American Bar Association… ABA accreditation does not extend to any program supporting any other degree granted by the law school. Rather the content and requirements of those degrees, such a s an LLM, are created by the law school itself and do not reflect any judgment by the ABA accrediting bodies regarding the quality of the program.[91]

The sentiments of Chief Justice Randall T. Shepard were also echoed recently by ABA.[92] And we have already examined ABA's sentiments. It appears ABA simply endorsed fully, and without reservations, the views of Chief Justice Randall T. Shepard. According to Chief Justice Randall T. Shepard,

> "Moreover, admission requirements for such programs (that is, the LLM and SJD programs), particularly with regard to foreign students, vary from school to school,

> and are not evaluated through the ABA accreditation process. The ABA reviews post-JD degree programs only to determine whether the offering of such post-JD program would have an adverse impact on the law school's ability to maintain its accreditation for the JD program. If no adverse impact is indicated, the ABA 'acquiesces' in the law school's decision to offer the non-JD program and degree. We bring this issue to your renewed attention because of the striking increase in the number of post-JD degree programs offered by the ABA accredited law schools and because a post-JD degree from an ABA accredited law school can in some jurisdictions qualify an applicant to sit for the bar examinations. It appears therefore, that some jurisdictions have assumed that a program leading to the granting of a post-JD degree in an ABA approved law school has been evaluated and approved by the ABA. This is an invalid assumption. The ABA Accreditation process does not evaluate in any way whether the post-JD degree program provides the basic legal principles and skills determined to be necessary to provide the public with the assurance of a competent practicing bar. Thus, we think it important to remind you that, unlike the JD degree bestowed by an ABA accredited law school which carries the indicia that the holder of that degree has completed a course of study imparting standards entitling him or her to engage in the practice of law, a post-JD degree from an ABA accredited law school has not received any approval for its content or any other requirement for the degree.[93]

Against the foregoing, it is evident that the JD is the sole degree that attracts professional accreditation from ABA. As a result, in the eyes of many American trained lawyers, the JD carries more prestige than the LLM and SJD degrees. Unlike many law schools in the Commonwealth, some US law schools do not even offer post-JD qualifications. Only a limited number of American universities offer the LLM and SJD degrees. An obvious reason behind this anomaly is that the JD degree is the only ABA accredited law degree that is offered in the US.[94] By contrast, the content and requirements of the LLM and SJD degrees in the US, as Chief Justice Randall T. Shepard points out,[95] are created by the respective law schools themselves and do not reflect any judgment by the ABA accrediting bodies regarding the quality of such degrees. So, where are we left with the American LLM and SJD degrees?

One view is that if we focus only on the 'name' of the university granting the LLM or SJD degrees, then the prestige of the JD will be watered down. The JD will be seen as standing lower on the echelons of academe. Advocates of this view often question ABA's *locus standi* in issuing statements on the quality of post-JD degrees, arguing that, after all, what matters is not the letters after your name, but the name after those letters; meaning, all that matters is the name of the university where you went to, and not the type of degree you got or whether that degree is even accredited. This view is premised on the assumption that since accreditation is a voluntary process whereby a university submits its programme to a private body for institutional recognition and approval, there is no need to worry about the lack of ABA accreditation that American LLM and SJD programmes suffer. Proponents of this theory often argue that, who cares about what ABA thinks? But law schools in the US, including the American legal profession, do care about what ABA thinks. That is why almost all law schools in the US have at one point or another sought or considered seeking ABA accreditation—because they do care about what ABA thinks. So, the final view of ABA, regarding whether or not a particular law school or degree programme is accredited, carries the day. We would be pursuing a red herring if we were to try to spin the argument around, agitating that after all ABA does not run law schools and, as a consequence, ABA has no legitimate ground to issue statements on the quality of post-JD degrees. As explained above, American law schools, including the legal profession, do listen to ABA and they do care about what ABA thinks.

A related argument is that if we choose to recognise the process of ABA accreditation, and view such a process as an important element in the validation of academic degrees and institutions, the JD degree will retain its prestigious status over the LLM and SJD degrees. This theory appears to be more persuasive to many American trained lawyers. The theory explains, perhaps, why the LLM and SJD degrees attract mainly foreign students and why these degrees are, generally, shunned by most people who have the JD degree: as Chief Justice Randall T. Shepard observes, the content and requirements of the LLM and SJD degrees are created by the law schools themselves and do not reflect any judgment by the ABA accrediting bodies regarding the quality of the programmes.[96]

Interestingly, some American law schools have tried to market and promote their LLM programmes in a manner that suggests that LLMs for foreign-trained lawyers are somewhat different in scope and focus from LLMs for JD degree holders.[97] A case in point is Harvard Law School's view of its LLM degree programme. According to Harvard Law School,

> For students who hold a J.D. from a law school in the United States or Puerto Rico, the emphasis is slightly different. For these students, the LL.M. degree is designed as preparation for a career in law teaching. These students are provided the opportunity to take a step back and relate the doctrinal areas in which they previously concentrated to broader intellectual, social and cultural traditions; and pursue an extended writing project. Thus students from the United States and Puerto Rico must take at least one course in legal theory or jurisprudence and write either the LL.M. paper or the LL.M. thesis.[98]

But, the LLM does not gain a stronger reputation professionally just because 'for students who hold a J.D. from a law school in the United States or Puerto Rico, the emphasis is slightly different.'

If anything, a good number of JD degree holders often shun the LLM and SJD degree programmes. Why? This is a fundamental question that foreign-trained lawyers ought to ask themselves.[102]

Chapter 4

Bringing Accreditation of Law Schools on Board

Although in the UK, like the US, there is no legal requirement that a university should be accredited for it to be recognised,[99] the concept of accreditation carries more weight and public approval in the US than it does in the UK. Reasons for these differences are both historical and ideological. Here, suffice it to say many law schools in the Commonwealth are members of the Commonwealth Legal Education Association (CLEA).[100] However, unlike ABA, CLEA is not a regulator of Bar admissions or law practice. The equivalent of the Americans' ABA in the UK is the Law Society, although the latter body is not as concerned with the accreditation of academic degrees as ABA.[101] As the Law Society points out, "The Law Society is the representative and regulatory body for solicitors of England and Wales."[102]

4.1 Commonwealth Legal Education Association

At the Commonwealth level, CLEA has been in existence since its inception in December 1971.[103] The objectives of CLEA are to foster high standards of legal education and research in Commonwealth countries, to build up contacts between interested individuals and organisations and to disseminate information and literature concerning legal education and research.[104] CLEA has four chapters carrying out activities on a region-wide basis; the South-East Asian Chapter, the Southern African Chapter, the Caribbean Chapter and the West African Chapter. In addition, there is a CLEA UK Committee.[105] The Association is a registered charity and receives funding from, amongst others, the Commonwealth Foundation.[106] Membership is open to individuals, schools of law and other institutions concerned with legal education and research.[107] The Association enjoys the support of a distinguished list of patrons from various Commonwealth countries.[108] The Association's chief activities include events and conferences, curriculum development and a publications programme.[109]

4.2 Association of American Law Schools

The US equivalent of CLEA is the Association of American Law Schools (AALS). Founded in 1900, AALS is a non-profit association of approximately 166 law schools.[110] In the US, a law school is eligible to apply for membership of AALS after it has offered five years of instruction and has graduated its third class. The purpose of AALS is 'the improvement of the legal profession through legal education.'[111] AALS serves as the learned society for law teachers and is legal education's principal representative to the Federal US Government and to other national higher education organisations and learned societies.[112]

In the UK alone, an organisation that has goals similar to those of AALS is the British Association of Law Teachers (ALT).[113]

The UK's ALT is made up of law teachers from all sectors and has for over 35 years played an active role at the heart of legal education.[114] ALT now has an international membership and maintains close links with other national and international organisations pursuing similar interests.[115]

4.3 Association of African Universities and Association of Commonwealth Universities

In Africa, some Commonwealth African law schools, apart from being members of CLEA, belong to universities that are members of both the Association of African Universities (AAU)[116] and the Association of Commonwealth Universities (ACU).[117] ACU is the oldest international association of universities in the world.[118] Indeed, ACU is a voluntary society founded in 1913. It is registered as a Charity and is governed by its member institutions through an elected council. Among its key activities are:

- assisting members to develop the capacity of their human resources
- promoting, through several programs, the movement of academic and administrative staff and of students from one country of the Commonwealth to another
- providing information about universities and about issues of relevance to them
- hosting a higher education management consultancy service
- organizing meetings of various kinds.[119]

Closely related to ACU, AAU is the apex body and principal forum for consultation, exchange of information and cooperation among universities in Africa. The headquarters of AAU is in Accra, Ghana, and the institution celebrated its thirty-fifth anniversary on November 12, 2002.[120] The objectives of AAU are as follows:[121]

- To promote interchange, contact and cooperation among university institutions in Africa;
- To collect, classify and disseminate information on higher education and research, particularly in Africa;
- To promote cooperation among African Institutions in curriculum development, and in the determination of equivalence of degrees;
- To encourage increased contracts between its members and the international academic world;
- To study and make known the educational and related needs of African university institutions and, as far as practicable, to coordinate the means whereby those needs may be met;
- To encourage the development and wider use of African languages; and,
- To organize, encourage and support seminars and conferences between African university teachers, administrators and others dealing with problems of higher education in Africa.

4.4 PRIVATE AND PUBLIC UNIVERSITIES AND THE QUESTION OF THEIR ACCREDITATION

Overall, unlike the US, the UK has one private university.[122] The rest of British universities are public institutions. By contrast, in the US, there are several thousands of private universities.[123] Obviously, with such a structure of higher education, the US is more prone to the notorious system of aggressive ranking and accreditation of universities than the UK.

Further, the US, unlike the UK, has several private and non-State approved agencies that claim to have the mandate to accredit universities and university programmes.[124] Some of these US accrediting agencies are dubious organisations that specialise in fraudulent activities.[125] Comparatively, in Australia, Canada and many other Commonwealth countries, some universities are set up, and given recognition, by an Act of Parliament.[126] In these countries, the concept of accreditation does not carry the same weight and public approval that it carries in the US. Often, the issue of accreditation only comes up in relation to professional programmes that prepare individuals to practice a profession. Examples here may include accreditation of a medical school by the country's medical council, accreditation of a law school by the Bar admission authorities, or accreditation of an accountancy degree programme by the country's professional accountancy body. In Canada, for example, the Association of Canadian Medical Colleges postulates:

> Canadian medical schools are jointly accredited by the Committee on Accreditation of Canadian Medical Schools (CACMS) and the Liaison Committee on Medical Education (LCME, US). These bodies are established by the profession and are independent of government... Accreditation is a four-step process beginning with an institutional self-study (often costing $CAD 150,000) 12 to 18 months before the site survey, completion of an institutional database three months prior to the survey, visitation by an ad hoc survey team and finally consideration of the survey report by the CACMS and LCME leading to a decision re: accreditation... Six areas are considered: objectives, governance, administration, educational program for the MD degree, medical students, and resources for the education program.[127]

In other Commonwealth countries, a royal charter is one other instrument that provides for the setting up of and the granting of formal recognition to universities.[128]And, generally speaking, the process of accreditation, whenever it comes up in Commonwealth countries, is often not a function of private accrediting bodies. A major reason for this development is that, unlike in the US, there are not many private law schools or universities in Commonwealth countries and a culture of having privately owned law schools is simply not there. Therefore, in as far as international recognition of academic credentials is concerned, the standing of the LLM and PhD (law) degrees from a decent and credible university in the Commonwealth is arguably better than that of the unaccredited American LLM and SJD degrees. As Phillips and Pugh observe, regarding the standard of a US Doctorate when compared with a British Doctorate:

> A major difference in the United States is that each student has a thesis committee made up of three members of academic staff, instead of a single supervisor. In practice, the chair of the committee becomes the leading supervisor…There are, though, two other supervisors who may intervene in the work of the student, often at quite an advanced stage. There are often the problems between colleagues that we have mentioned when discussing joint supervisors. It should be noted that three members of the thesis committee constitute the examining board, and the degree is awarded if they are satisfied that the student has carried out the approved thesis proposal. There are no external examiners involved, which means that standards vary widely between universities and between disciplines within each university. In our view, the American system in detail has little to offer British practice, other than the useful concept of the doctoral programme itself.[129]

4.5 Some Shortcomings of the British PhD System

Although a British *PhD by thesis* points to deeper and more meaningful research methodologically than its American counterpart, the *PhD by coursework and dissertation*, the idea, in the UK, of permitting some students who obtain a first class or upper second class on their Bachelors degree to proceed directly to a PhD raises a number of concerns.[130] The argument that a PhD student in the UK enrols initially as a Master of Philosophy degree (MPhil) student before he or she is later confirmed as a PhD student does not resolve matters. The MPhil degree is a research degree and it does not equip the student (who has not undertaken a taught Masters degree) with adequate conceptual and theoretical grounding in a particular field of knowledge. The situation is even more worrying with the coming on board of the new universities in the UK.[131] These institutions were polytechnics until 1992 when the British Government granted them the status of universities.[132] It is not entirely clear if most of these new universities have been able to raise their academic standards to the level of the older British universities. And a quick look at league tables in the UK reveals that the former polytechnics have consistently received lower ratings than the older British universities. Perhaps, one consolation for the former British polytechnics is that in the US there are hundreds more of such institutions with low academic standards compared to the smaller number of elite American universities with high academic standards. Against this background, let us now turn to look at related academic programmes which also impact on the development of legal education.

4.6 Concept of a *PhD by Submission of Published Work*

Although the idea of a *PhD by submission of published work* is well recognised in most Commonwealth countries, including New Zealand,[133] Australia[134] and the UK,[135] the standards of this doctoral programme have not been harmonised across universities and countries.[136] And, in the US, most American universities have shied away from the idea of awarding PhDs by published work.

However, lately, the University of Columbia Law School has stated that its JSD degree (Doctor of the Science of Law) is awarded to persons who have completed with distinction an approved program of study, research, and writing, and that the JSD dissertation 'can take the form of a unified work or *a set of three articles* with a unifying essay.'[137] Similarly, the University of Pennsylvania Law School observes as follows:

> The principal requirement for the degree of Doctor of Juridical Science (S.J.D.) is a dissertation that makes an original and substantive contribution to legal scholarship and an oral defense of that dissertation. This contemplates a book or extended monograph reflecting intensive and creative research with respect to a specific topic, problem, or area of law. The work, both in content and form, must be of publishable quality and normally must have been submitted and accepted for publication either as an extensive article (or series of articles) in a law review or a book.[138]

By contrast, in Commonwealth Africa, although many universities may have regulations permitting the award of a *PhD by submission of published work*, it is almost inconceivable that a good number of these African universities can confer such an esteemed degree on a citizen of their country without going through a protracted drama of petty jealousies and personalisation of issues.

4.7 The American *PhD by Coursework and Dissertation*

In contrast to most PhD programmes in Commonwealth countries, the taught component of the American PhD (i.e., comprehensives) brings about monotony, especially where a candidate has already undertaken a Masters degree by taught coursework in the field of specialisation or the discipline where he or she intends to carry out the doctoral research. Indeed, what purpose does further coursework serve here? There are probably three main hypotheses that might help to explain why most PhD students in the US have to undertake further coursework before they can embark on doctoral research, and these are:

(a) either the Masters degree programme that the PhD student completed before registering for a PhD was not strong enough academically, and his or her PhD dissertation committee is of the view that he or she would benefit from undertaking additional coursework,
(b) the student has switched disciplines at doctoral level, abandoning his or her specialisation at Masters degree level, and would therefore benefit from undertaking some coursework in the new field of specialisation, or
(c) the student's PhD dissertation committee is of the view the student is not strong enough academically to indulge directly into writing his or her PhD dissertation without undertaking some additional coursework.

Experience, generally, has shown that many universities hardly articulate publicly and fully the rationale behind the requirement that a PhD student should first undertake some coursework before embarking on doctoral research. Here, academic conventions and traditions are the mantra of the day in the absence of a proper discourse to explain why things are done in a certain way. Some universities in Europe and Africa have, however, started developing their PhD programmes along the lines of the American PhD by coursework and dissertation.[139]

4.8 Higher Doctorates in the UK and the Commonwealth

Generally, the notion of Doctorates that are higher than a PhD—it would matter less that the PhD was undertaken by research or coursework or submission of published work—is one that is rare in the United States and Canada, but more established in the UK,

Ireland and Commonwealth countries.[140] Examples of higher Doctorates include the following:[141]

(a) Doctor of Divinity/Divinitatis Doctor (DD);
(b) Doctor of Civil Law (DCL);
(c) Doctor of Laws/Legum Doctor (LLD);
(d) Doctor of Medicine/Medicinæ Doctor (DM or MD, i.e., earned at a medical school outside the US, such as a British medical school, that does not use the title of 'Doctor of Medicine' for its first-professional degree in medicine);
(e) Doctor of Letters/Litterarum Doctor (DLitt or Litt.D);
(f) Doctor of Science/Scientiæ Doctor (DSc. or Sc.D.);
(g) Doctor of Music/Musicæ Doctor (DMus. or Mus.D);
(h) Doctor of Technology (DTech.);
(i) Doctor of Governance (DGov); and,
(j) Doctor of the University (DUniv.; usually honorary).

Then, the degree of Doctor of Juridical Science (SJD or JSD), awarded mainly by top US law schools and some Australian, Canadian and Chinese law schools,[142] like the degree of Doctor of Engineering (DEng. or Eng.D.), is considered by some commentators and educationists as comparable to the PhD.[143] The SJD, however, should not be compared with or confused for a higher Doctorate simply because the title of the first-professional degree below the SJD—that is, the Juris Doctor (JD)—carries the word 'Doctor.' We have already established that a JD is not a true Doctorate and that it is comparable and equivalent to an LLB degree.

As a general rule, in the hierarachy of university qualifications, a higher Doctorate is a senior Doctorate. A higher Doctorate ranks ahead of a PhD and an SJD. Today, it is not common to find someone with a higher Doctorate. The requirements and academic standards for admission to a higher Doctorate are extremely high.

As a result, higher Doctorates have become very rare. Even in jurisdictions outside the common law, higher Doctorates are becoming increasingly rare.

In practice, the award of a higher Doctorate is reserved only for exceptional cases where there is evidence of sustained scholarship over the years, constituting an authoritative body of knowledge that is publicly available in the form of published scholarly books and refereed articles in leading academic journals. And these publications must be of a scholarly standing far above that of a PhD or a mere professorship.

At many universities, a higher Doctorate can be awarded in a discipline such as law. Where a higher Doctorate is awarded for scholarly contrbutions in law, it is normally referred to as the degree of Doctor of Laws (LLD).[144] To be specific,

> In the United Kingdom, Australia, and New Zealand, the degree is a higher doctorate usually awarded on the basis of exceptionally insightful and distinctive publications that contain significant and original contributions to the study of law. Some universities, such as the University of Oxford, award a Doctor of Civil Law degree instead. In Canada, LL.D and Doctor of Civil Law degrees are awarded as substitute of Ph.D. in law. In South Africa, the LL.D. is awarded by many university law faculties as the highest degree in law, based upon research and completion of a Ph.D. equivalent dissertation.[145] The LL.D. may also be awarded as an honorary degree based upon a person's contributions to society. In Malta, the LL.D. is a post-graduate doctoral degree requiring at least three years of full time study at the University of Malta, Malta's one and only university. Students are required to complete coursework in a number of core areas, as well as 'submit a thesis which shall be an original work on the approved subject or other contribution to the knowledge showing that he/she has carried out sufficient research therein.[146]

By contrast, in Commonwealth Africa, although a number of universities may have regulations governing the award of higher Doctorates, it is almost inconceivable that some of these universities would confer a higher Doctorate on a citizen of their country without the experience turning into protracted drama of petty jealousies and personalisation of issues. If anything, most capable academics in Africa would rather not apply for a higher Doctorate knowing fully well the politics that could surround such an attempt.

Chapter 5

The Role of University League Tables

Over the years, the US system of higher education has enjoyed the ranking of universities using various formulas and indexes. Although a recent phenomenon in the UK, the ranking of universities has also gained momentum there. In both the UK and the US, different rating agencies, persons and newspapers keep generating all sorts of university league tables. These tables are generated almost every year, highlighting universities that are believed to be academically stronger than others.

5.1 Criteria for Formulating League Tables

According to the Institute of Higher Education, Shanghai Jiao Tong University, which ranks universities in Europe, Asia, and the Americas annually,

> We rank universities by several indicators of academic or research performance, including alumni and staff winning Nobel Prizes and Fields Medals, highly cited researchers, articles published in Nature and Science, articles indexed in major citation indices, and the per capita academic performance of an institution. For each indicator, the highest scoring institution is assigned a score of 100, and other institutions are calculated as a percentage of the top score. The distribution of data for each indicator is examined for any significant distorting effect; standard statistical techniques are used to adjust the indicator if necessary. Scores for each indicator are weighted as shown below to arrive at a final overall score for an institution. The highest scoring institution is assigned a score of 100, and other institutions are calculated as a percentage of the top score. An institution's rank reflects the number of institutions that sit above it.[148]

However, Leyn argues forcefully against the idea of ranking of universities, as he points out that:

> We seem to have a never-ending fondness for ranking. We rank schools, we rank hotels, we rank the cost of living in different countries, and so on. There is something about the competitive streak in human nature that makes us want to compare ourselves with everybody else. The Shanghai Jiao Tong University ranked the top 500 universities in the world, and published their findings in September 2004. Their methodology involved looking at four main criteria: (a) the quality of education (alumni winning Nobel or Field Prizes); (b) the quality of the faculty (staff with Nobel or Field Prizes, highly cited researchers); (c) the research output (articles published in top journals e.g., Nature, Science, etc.; articles cited in Science or Social Science Citation Indices); and, (d) the size of institution (academic performance with respect to size of institution). The Times Higher Education Supplement published its ranking of the top 200 universities in the world on 5 November 2004. They explained that

> their ranking was based on: (a) Peer Review (by 1,300 academics in 88 countries); (b) Research impact (calculated by measuring citations per faculty member); and, (c) International orientation (the number of international students and faculty members).[149]

Highlighting some of the contradictions inherent in the ranking of universities, Leyn adds:

> Ranking of the World's Top Ten Universities 2004:
>
> *Times Higher Education Supplement (THES)*
>
> 1. Harvard University
> 2. University of California, Berkeley
> 3. Massachusetts Institute of Technology (MIT)
> 4. California Institute of Technology
> 5. Oxford University
> 6. Cambridge University
> 7. Stanford University
> 8. Yale University
> 9. Princeton University
> 10. ETH Zurich
>
> *Shanghai Jiao Tong University (SJTU)*
>
> 1. Harvard University
> 2. Stanford University
> 3. Cambridge University
> 4. University of California, Berkeley
> 5. Massachusetts Institute of Technology (MIT)
> 6. California Institute of Technology
> 7. Princeton University
> 8. Oxford University
> 9. Columbia University
> 10. Chicago University.

> The criteria used for ranking must perforce be arbitrary. Thus, not unnaturally, people's eyebrows will be raised when they see this list. And one can forever debate whether or not this university is really better than that. Which ranking list is the more accurate? I don't know...[150]

According to Leyn, the SJTU survey places an inordinate weight on individual achievements (for example, Nobel and Field Prize-winners will greatly influence a university's ranking, yet such prizes are awarded long after the research has been completed, and that placing emphasis on individual achievements tends to discriminate unfairly against newer universities) whereas the THES analysis relies on peer review quite heavily such that the older universities would have an advantage because they often have a number of famous professors, many of whom have written books used by undergraduates and postgraduate students (thus newer universities would be disadvantaged by this system, too).[151]

Generally, the preparation of some league tables will concentrate on the ranking of universities based on the strength of a particular discipline or course offering. Others concentrate on the ranking of universities based on, *inter alia*, the research output of academic staff. Then, there are also those that concentrate on using such criteria as the teaching quality of academic staff at a university, the number of faculty members at a university, the employability or marketability of graduates of a particular university, the expenditure of a university's library system when acquiring research materials yearly, the availability of student accommodation on university campus, and the prestige of academic schools that offer first-professional degrees, such as a university's Medical School and Law School. Whichever way, league tables are often generated by private bodies and individuals and these league tables do not necessarily reflect the view of the Government. As ABA observes, in the case of the US:

5. Rating of Law Schools

No rating of law schools beyond the simple statement of their accreditation status is attempted or advocated by the official organizations in legal education. Qualities that make one kind of school good for one student may not be as important to another. The American Bar Association and its Section of Legal Education and Admissions to the Bar have issued disclaimers of any law school rating system. Prospective law students should consider a variety of factors in making their choice among schools.[152]

5.2 Ivy League Universities and University League Tables in the US

In the US, for one reason or another, Ivy League Universities—that is, Brown University, Harvard University, Columbia University, Yale University, Cornell University, Dartmouth College, University of Pennsylvania, and Princeton University—have always enjoyed comfortable positions on league tables.[153] Examining the term *Ivy League*, Princeton University explains:

> *Ivy League* is the name generally applied to eight universities (Brown, Columbia, Cornell, Dartmouth, Harvard, Pennsylvania, Princeton, and Yale) that over the years have had common interests in scholarship as well as in athletics.[154]

According to Princeton University,

> Stanley Woodward, *New York Herald Tribune* sports writer, coined the phrase in the early thirties. In 1936 the undergraduate newspapers of these universities simultaneously ran an editorial advocating the formation of an 'Ivy League,' but the first move toward this end was not taken until 1945. In that year, the eight presidents entered into an agreement 'for the purpose of *reaffirming* their intention of continuing intercollegiate football in such a way as to maintain the values of the game, while keeping it in

> fitting proportion to the main purposes of academic life.' To achieve this objective two inter-university committees were appointed: one, made up primarily of the college deans, was to administer rules of eligibility; the other, composed of the athletic directors, was to establish policies on the length of the playing season and of preseason practice, operating budgets, and related matters. Two other inter-university committees on admission and financial aid were added later. As President Dodds pointed out at the time, the general principles agreed on by the eight universities were essentially the same as those set forth in the Harvard-Yale-Princeton Presidents' Agreement of 1916.[155]

5.3 Best Ranked Law Schools in the US

A recently drawn league table of the top twenty law schools in the US reveals the following:

Figure 5.3 Top 20 US Law Schools based on Faculty Quality, 2003–04

Rank	School (number of faculty)	Mean	Median
1.	Yale University (53)	4.8	5.0
2.	Harvard University (80)	4.7	5.0
3.	University of Chicago (35)	4.7	5.0
4.	Stanford University (40)	4.5	4.5
5.	Columbia University (61)	4.3	4.5
6.	New York University (82)	4.3	4.5
7.	University of California, Berkeley (54)	4.2	4.5
8.	University of Michigan, Ann Arbor (52)	4.1	4.0
9.	University of Texas, Austin (73)	4.1	4.0
10.	University of Virginia (60)	4.0	4.0
11.	University of Pennsylvania (45)	3.9	4.0
12.	Georgetown University (87)	3.8	4.0
13.	University of Southern California (43)	3.8	4.0
14.	Cornell University (32)	3.7	3.75
15.	Northwestern University (50)	3.7	4.0
16.	University of California, Los Angeles (62)	3.7	4.0
17.	Duke University (47)	3.5	3.5

Continued

18.	Vanderbilt University (39)	3.4	3.5
19.	Boston University (54)	3.3	3.5
20.	University of Iowa (40)	3.3	3.5

Source: Educational Quality ranking of US Law School 2003–2004, available Online at: http://www.utexas.edu/law/faculty/bleiter/rankings/rankings03.html, visited on January 22, 2004.

5.4 Russell Group of Universities and University League Tables in the UK

In recent years, the UK has also responded with its own version of an Ivy League system of universities. The equivalent of the Ivy League system in the UK is the *Russell Group of Universities*. As Wikipedia Encyclopedia points out:

> The Russell Group of Universities is a self-selected group of large research-led British universities, with 18 of the 19 members being in the top 20 in terms of size of research funding. The group is often presented in the media as a kind of Ivy League, representing the interests of Britain's prestigious universities. However, unlike the Ivy League, all of the Russell Group universities are state-funded. The confusion of 'large' with 'prestigious' has also sometimes led to assumptions that some smaller universities, such as York, Durham and St Andrews are members, when they are not.

The following UK universities, listed alphabetically, constitute the 19 members of the Russell Group of Universities:[157]

- Cardiff University
- Imperial College, London
- King's College, London
- London School of Economics
- University College London
- University of Birmingham

- University of Bristol
- University of Cambridge
- University of Edinburgh
- University of Glasgow
- University of Leeds
- University of Liverpool
- University of Manchester
- University of Newcastle upon Tyne
- University of Nottingham
- University of Oxford
- University of Sheffield
- University of Southampton
- University of Warwick

There is no doubt that Oxbridge universities—that is, Oxford and Cambridge—whose trans-Atlantic rivals in the US are Harvard and Yale, sit comfortably in the Russell Group of Universities.[158] However, an important caveat must be mentioned here, regarding the correlation between Ivy League Universities and the Russell Group of Universities, on the one hand, and the respective ranking of universities in the US and the UK, on the other. As in the case of Ivy League Universities, not all Russell Group of Universities have faired well on university league tables. In the case of the Russell Group of Universities, only a few universities, such as Oxford, Cambridge, Imperial College, Warwick and London School of Economics, have maintained some consistency in being ranked highly on the university league tables.

Similarly, in the US, Harvard, Yale, Princeton and Columbia seem to be the better of the Ivy League. That said, an interesting feature of the US Ivy League system is that although Stanford University is not part of the Ivy League, it continues to enjoy a much stronger academic reputation, both within the US and internationally, than most Ivy League Universities.

5.5 Best Ranked Law Schools in the UK

In the UK, a recently drawn league table of the top twenty British law schools reveals the following:

Figure 5.5 Top 20 UK Law Schools (compiled by the Guardian) in May, 2002

	Institution	Guardian teaching score/100	Teaching inspection score/24	Spend score/10	Student:staff ratio score/6	Job prospects score/6	Value added score/10	Reputation score/6
1.	Oxford	88.63	23	10	6	4	2.50	6
2.	Warwick	88.40	23	8	6	6	2.25	6
3.	University College London	87.72	23	8	6	6	1.50	6
4.	Cambridge	87.27	23	8	5	5	3.00	6
5.	London School of Economics	87.27	23	10	6	3	2.00	6
6.	Essex	86.59	23	8	5	6	2.25	5
7.	Bristol	86.13	23	6	4	6	3.75	6
8.	Nottingham	85.90	23	7	4	6	2.50	6
9.	School of Oriental and African Studies	85.68	23	8	5	4	3.25	5
10.	Manchester	85.45	23	7	5	5	2.00	6
11.	King's College London	84.09	23	6	6	3	2.50	6
12.	East Anglia	82.49	23	4	4	6	2.75	5
13.	Durham	82.27	23	4	5	5	1.50	6
14.	Leicester	82.27	23	6	4	5	1.50	5
15.	Northumbria at Newcastle	82.04	23	4	4	6	2.25	5
16.	Sheffield	82.04	23	5	4	4	2.25	6
17.	Queen's Belfast	81.36	23	6	3	4	1.50	6
18.	Oxford Brookes	81.13	23	6	4	3	2.25	5
19.	Birmingham	80.68	20	10	6	5	1.75	6
20.	Wales, Aberystwyth	80.45	23	5	3	4	2.50	5

Source: The Guardian Unlimited: EducationGuardian.co.uk, available Online at: http://education.guardian.co.uk/higher/unitable/0,11985,723568,00.html, visited on January 22, 2004.

5.6 A Financial Dimension to University League Tables

In general, the system of ranking universities and university faculties has a marketing function. Prospective students tend to apply to universities ranked highly on league tables. Also, the information set out in league tables can persuade prospective funding bodies to channel their financial resources to top research universities. And in as far as raising funds for research and educational purposes is concerned, top US universities have faired much better than their British counterparts. For example, looking at law schools alone, we find that tuition fees at top US law schools far outstrip tuition fees at most UK law schools. Yet, tuition fees constitute an important source of revenue for most universities worldwide. Suffice it to say that the reasons why UK universities appear under-funded, when compared with their US counterparts, are several. They include micro-economic and macro-economic variables which are beyond the scope of the book. Overall, a number of UK universities have been struggling to raise finances and this is putting a major financial strain on the British Government to continue subsidising higher education.[159]

5.7 Ranking of Universities in Commonwealth Africa

Within Commonwealth Africa, there is hardly any evidence of ranking of universities. South Africa seems to have experimented with some rankings of some sort, but these rankings are not widely publicised. However, Internet Lab (*Observatorio de Ciencia y Tecnologia en Internet*), a research body of the Spanish Research Council, postulates that the following represents a standing of the top 30 universities in Africa.[160]

Figure. 5.7 Top 30 African universities (compiled by InternetLab)

The InternetLab Ranking of 30 Top African Universities

Rank	*University*	*Country*	*World Rank*
1.	University of Cape Town	South Africa	398
2.	Universiteit Stellenbosch	South Africa	566
3.	Universiteit van Pretoria—University of Pretoria	South Africa	718
4.	University of the Witwatersrand	South Africa	720
5.	Rhodes University	South Africa	738
6.	University of South Africa	South Africa	1,449
7.	University of the Western Cape	South Africa	1,553
8.	American University in Cairo	Egypt	1,826
9.	Noordwes Universiteit—North West University	South Africa	1,857
10.	University of KwaZulu-Natal	South Africa	2,214
11.	University of Johannesburg	South Africa	2,323
12.	University of the Free State	South Africa	2,369
13.	Université de La Reunion	France	2,387
14.	Nelson Mandela Metropolitan University	South Africa	2,542
15.	University of Dar Es Salam	Tanzania	2,819
16.	University of Zimbabwe	Zimbabwe	3,072
17.	Al Akhawayn University in Ifrane	Morocco	3,174
18.	Cape Technikon	South Africa	3,414
19.	University of Mauritius	Mauritius	3,682
20.	University of Zululand	South Africa	3,724

Source: F. Sabatini (ed) (University of Rome La Sapienza and University of Cassino), "Social Capital Gateway: Resources for the Study of Social Capital," available Online at: http://www.socialcapitalgateway.org/eng-rankingafrica.htm, visited on October 29, 2006 (extracted from the web-site of InternetLab (Observatorio de Ciencia y Tecnologia en Internet)).

The list presented above is dominated by South African universities. Yet, a number of these South African universities, especially the former polytechnics and the former Bantustan universities, were lesser known a decade ago compared to the older and well-established names in the likes of the University of Ghana, the

University of Ibadan, Makerere University, the University of Zambia, the University of Nairobi, the University of Nigeria and Ahmadu Bello University. So, what has been happening to these older universities outside South Africa? Is it that the league table presented above is biased in favour of universities located in stronger economies, such as South Africa? Or is it that South African universities have taken advantage of the country's strong economy and have utilised effectively the availability of such valuable resources as information technology, human capital and finance to develop South Africa's higher education system?

Overall, Nigeria and South Africa have the largest number of universities in Commonwealth Africa. While South African universities seem to be more popular than Nigerian ones, especially with regard to institutional credibility and the degree of government funding accorded to universities, there are many other well-developed universities across Commonwealth Africa. However, the greatest threat that these institutions face today is limited funding from the national budget. As an off-shoot, there has been mass exodus of human capital from these institutions, resulting, in part, in the over-stretched use of minimum resources. This, in turn, affects the quality of education. Research, too, cannot thrive where academic and research institutions are poorly funded. Indeed, where research is not encouraged and supported financially there is often a mismatch between research outputs and the priority areas of national development.

5.8 Private Universities (or Law Schools) in Africa

In Commonwealth Africa, there are very few privately owned universities. Even Nigeria and South Africa, boasting of the largest number of universities in Commonwealth Africa, do not have as many privately owned universities as the US. The closest competitor to the US is, perhaps, India.

By contrast, and as noted earlier, all UK universities, except for one privately owned university, the University of Buckingham, are public institutions. Commonwealth African countries have followed the British model. Therefore, the question of private bodies having to accredit universities in Commonwealth Africa does not even arise since most universities are not privately owned, but funded by the State. Admittedly, there is a fiscal cost on the national budget to financing the operations of State-funded universities. In a number of countries, the debate is looming on whether to encourage the privatisation of State-funded educational institutions. Arguments pointing to the cost of financing these institutions have been buttressed by dictates of the market economy favouring competition in order to improve quality and promote efficiency in delivery of educational products. The university league tables in the US and the UK are evidence of the market economy dictates that champion competition in higher education. There is an implicit assumption that competition will lead to efficiency in the delivery of a quality educational service. But, can the poor people of Africa afford privatised and unsubsidised university education? What impact will privatisation of higher institutions of learning have on the poor masses of Africa? And, will there be any improvement in the quality of education?

5.9 A Notable Function of Education in Many Parts of Africa

In many African countries, a large faction of the pubic believes that most academic degrees from the US, in contrast to degrees from British universities, are suspect and that they are too easily acquired. That said, some people acknowledge that there are some good American universities, such as those found in the top tier of US universities league tables. Such views are predicated on a number of factors that include the proliferation of dubious privately owned universities in the US.

Further, what worries many people in Africa is that some individuals that failed to gain admission to their local universities in Africa—not as a result of lack of financial sponsorship or because there was an outbreak of civil war, as some would want to claim, but because they did not meet the academic standards for admission to their home country universities—have found their way into some degree granting institution in the US. Lately, this unfortunate development has extended to the UK where a number of academically weak students from abroad have found their way into former polytechnics. There is a view in many parts of Africa that all it takes to get a degree in the US is money. And this view is now extending to some British degrees conferred by former UK polytechnics. By contrast, the older UK universities continue to enjoy much respect both at home and abroad. The only question that seems to resurface, time and again, relates to the quality of education at some former UK polytechnics.

Against this background, what are some of the factors that motivate many foreign students to leave their home country to pursue a first degree at a European university or an American university? Here are some helpful clues.

(a) Hypothetically, if an individual, say, from Kenya were to leave his or her home country to pursue a law degree at some 'small and lesser known' university, say, in India, it would quite obviously raise some eyebrows. The question here is: why did this person not study law at the University of Nairobi or any other recognised Kenyan university? Why did he or she have to go to a 'smaller and lesser known' university in India?

(b) Similarly, if an individual, say, from Zambia were to leave his or her home country to pursue a law degree at some

> 'small and lesser known' university, say, in South Africa, Botswana or Namibia, that would raise some eyebrows. Again, the question would be: why did this person not study law at the University of Zambia? Why did he or she have to go to a 'smaller and lesser known' university in South Africa, Botswana or Namibia?

There are often lesser burning issues associated with taking a recognisable Masters degree or a recognisable PhD from a decent university abroad in preference to pursuing postgraduate studies at a local African university. Here, our analysis extends to reasons why some African students travel abroad to seek a first degree.

Many arguments have been advanced by those that go to seek a first degree abroad that African universities are quite under-funded and that libraries at such institutions are often not well-stocked or that African universities are frequently closed down by politicians. Most of these reasons are valid, although such explanations do not tell us the full story why some Africans travel abroad to seek primary university education. A compelling argument here is that, under ordinary circumstances, an individual should start off with a first degree from his or her home country, unless he or she goes straight, for his or her first degree, to such famed places as Oxford, Harvard, Sorbonne, Princeton, Cambridge, Yale, Stanford, or Massachusetts Institute of Technology. In many cases, where an African student is from a country with a decent system of higher education, but he or she decides to undertake his or her university or college studies at some lowly placed and poorly regarded academic institution in the Western world, including some lesser known universities in Eastern Europe, Central Asia or South Asia, there is an implicit indication that such an individual did not make it to university in his or her home country. Indeed, such an individual could have faced insurmountable intellectual problems, and the home university could have deemed it not appropriate to admit and drag the student through university education. In short, judged by the academic standards in the student's home country, he or she was considered not bright enough to go to university. That said, we are mindful that there may be other reasons as well that help to shed light on why some Africans travel abroad to seek primary university education. But, such reasons are few and isolated.

5.10 Privatising University Education in Africa

In many parts of Commonwealth Africa, there is a perception that if you privatise universities even dull children whose parents are rich will be able to buy their way into university. In these parts of the world, university education does not—and is not expected to—have a commercial function. Indeed, there is a view that education is not a business venture that should be sold to the highest bidder. By contrast, education is seen by many as having an elitist and ethical function and that it should be earned by the best brains around. Lack of money or financial sponsorship, many people argue, should not be an impediment to acquiring a good education.

If, in admitting students to university, the admission authorities were to give greater weighting to financial means of a student than his or her academic prowess and intellectual abilities, then the quality of education would be compromised. At the end of the day, even dull children whose parents are rich would buy their way into university. In the US, this fear is not a deterrent. Many universities continue to struggle with the dilemma of upholding commercial-business motives or promoting higher ethical standards of academe. To a large extent, the LLM and SJD programmes in the US, lacking ABA accreditation and often dogged with inconsistencies in academic standards, are a subtle way in which American law schools are commercialising higher education.

Chapter 6

Policy Considerations for African Law Schools in the 21st Century

What is the way forward for law schools in Commonwealth Africa? Is there much to learn from academic programmes in the UK or the US? Let us take a more reasoned look.

6.1 Policy Recommendations

(a) A number of African law schools have well-developed and strong academic programmes at undergraduate level. The LLB degree programmes at these institutions rank at par with many LLB and JD programmes at top universities in the UK and the US.

On a broader scale of things, it would appear reasonable to assert that most African law schools have faired well on their undergraduate law degree programmes. If there are any improvements to be made, these would have to focus on, *inter alia*, increased funding to universities in order to promote research by academic staff, the introduction and addition of a few relevant and innovative modules on the LLB degree programmes so as to address some novel and emerging issues in the discourse of law and development, increased funding of staff development programmes, improved working conditions of academic staff generally so as to curb the alarming rate of human capital flight, increased funding of university libraries for the acquisition of modern academic literature, increased funding of universities in order to develop information technology for use at all faculties, and the need to limit the politicisation of African universities.

In general, the LLB curriculum of many law schools in Commonwealth Africa require law students to take first year courses from the social sciences before proceeding to law classes in the second year. This approach is unique to Africa and a few non-African countries. The approach should be encouraged in all other Commonwealth African law schools. The first year foundational courses serve the same purpose that the American pre-JD Bachelors degree serves.

(b) At postgraduate level, African universities and African law schools have something to learn from their counterparts in the West. It is not surprising, for example, that some LLM degree programmes in African universities, comprising both taught work and a dissertation of about 15,000 words, take an average of three to five years to complete. Yet, similar programmes can be completed in as little as 9 months at major universities in the UK and the US. There are several reasons to explain this anomaly.

First, with the exception of a few African universities, most universities in Africa run their postgraduate programmes as if these programmes are part-time programmes. This is so irrespective of the fact that university regulations suggest that the programme is full-time.

Secondly, the high turn-over rate of academic staff in-charge of postgraduate programmes, as these individuals pursue greener pastures elsewhere, often causes unnecessary delays and disruptions in the academic year.

Thirdly, some academics tasked with supervising Master of Laws (LLM) degree dissertations at universities in Africa have themselves never written an LLM dissertation or a PhD thesis. Indeed, some academics hold an LLM degree by coursework. There are many top US and UK universities whose LLM curriculum does not require all LLM students to write an LLM dissertation. And these LLM programmes have graduated many African academics. In such a situation, and if the LLM supervisor has not had much experience in supervising LLM or PhD students, he or she may experience conceptual and theoretical difficulties in pitching the student's dissertation at the right standard. Indeed, if the supervisor himself or herself never wrote an LLM dissertation or a PhD thesis, but simply undertook his or her LLM studies almost entirely by coursework, there is need to ensure that the supervisor has either published widely after his or her LLM, has undertaken a PhD thereafter, or has a wealth of experience supervising LLM dissertations or PhD theses. The idea here is that the supervisor himself or herself should be familiar with the intricacies of legal research and should not be experimenting on his or her students.

Fourth, some academics at African universities are busy shuttling between the university and the donor community, searching for donor-funded consultancy projects. Their argument is that life in Africa is tough and people have to make ends meet somehow. Consequently, there is hardly any serious commitment to research or to the improvement of postgraduate studies at many African universities. And neither can concepts such as that of a *PhD by submission of published work* or that of a *higher doctorate* be developed fully if a good number of academics at these institutions do not engage seriously in scholarly writing.

Fifth, a number of LLM students in Africa hardly reside on campus and they are often engaged in full-time work off-campus or they are engaged in full-time law practice. These dual professional roles usually make it difficult for these graduate students to commit wholly to full-time graduate law studies. Imagine a PhD student who is busy campaigning to be a member of parliament! And imagine a PhD student who masquerades as a contractor or a pastor! Some are even part-time businessmen, smuggling in cars from South Africa. What time would such students have to pursue PhD studies? Some of these matters have nothing to do with the economy and are, by contrast, part of a culture that is highly tolerant of indiscipline and laziness.

Sixth, the rampant political closures of some universities in Africa have contributed significantly to prolonged years of study.

Now, to redress the problems noted above, there is need to go back to recommendations spelt out earlier. To recapitulate, the following were some of the recommendations: increased funding to universities in order to promote research by academic members of staff; increased funding of staff development programmes at African universities; improved working conditions of academic staff, generally, so as to curb the alarming rate of human capital flight; increased funding of university libraries for the acquisition of modern academic literature; increased funding of universities to develop information technology for use at all faculties; and, the need to limit the politicisation of African universities.

Seventh, African universities would benefit more from administrators that have a clear vision of the function of a university in society and administrators who understand the role that a university plays in national development.

(c) Overall, the American LLM and SJD degree programmes do not have much to offer to African law schools and to the African experience. Similarly, the UK trend of permitting first class and upper second class LLB graduates to proceed directly to PhD programmes in law,[160] has limited attraction in Africa. Indeed, if African law schools are to maintain high academic standards, it is not advisable that they imitate their UK counterparts in the trend that permits some LLB graduates to proceed directly to a PhD programme. Preferably, an LLM degree, in a field closely related to the proposed PhD thesis, should be the ideal route for an aspiring PhD candidate. A number of British universities are now considering this route as a possible mandatory requirement in the near future.

(d) African universities and African law schools have to redefine the meaning of full-time postgraduate programmes in contrast to part-time degree programmes. Equally, the allocation of resources at these institutions has to match the competing and demanding interests of the academic programmes. It is costly to have programmes such an LLM run for four to five years and then have PhD students registered for eight to ten years. The quality of an academic programme, it should be emphasised, does not depend on the number of years that a student spends in school. Having said that, we concede that, sometimes, where there are personality clashes between a supervisor and his or her student that could cost the student heavily, in that he or she will not graduate in time.

(e) African universities and law schools must forge partnerships with institutions of higher learning in other parts of the world in order to promote international linkages of cultural exchange and foster collaborative research work.

(f) In addition, African universities and law schools need to explore and exploit potential partnerships with industry, tapping into private sector initiatives that could yield financial sponsorship of academic activities related to research and development.

6.2 Conclusion

This book has examined the extent to which African law schools can learn from some of the experiences of American and British law schools. It was noted that while the US and the UK have law schools that are a hundred or so years old, African countries have relatively young, but equally well-developed law schools. The book focused on various academic programmes offered at law schools in the US and the Commonwealth. It was demonstrated that American LLM and SJD degree programmes do not have much to offer to African law schools and that the trend in the UK of permitting some LLB graduates to proceed directly to PhD programmes has limited attraction in Africa.

Further, the book argued that a factor that has contributed to the shaping of the landscape of legal education in Commonwealth Africa was the intellectual interpretation of the law by the early judges, the civil servants and academics in the newly independent African States. The book explained, for example, how some academic programmes were constructed on the basis of the view of the world held by some expatriates.

Also examined in the book are concepts such as *years of pioneer professorships*, different types of Doctorate degrees, accreditation of law schools and law degrees, and university league tables. It was argued that the concept of accreditation of law schools and the concept of university league tables, though not fully developed and applied in Commonwealth Africa, are neither a necessity nor an imperative. But concepts such as those of a *PhD by published work* and a higher Doctorate should be revisited and implemented by Commonwealth African law schools.

NOTES

1. Zimbabwe, under President Robert Mugabe, decided in 2003 to withdraw its State membership from the Commonwealth, alleging, among other things, that Britain and its Western allies have continued to incite a racist and colonial mentality over the land dispute affecting most white farmers in Zimbabwe.
2. See M.L. Lehohla (the Chief Justice of Lesotho), "The Role of Customary Law in Developing Africa: the Lesotho position," (Washington DC: July 9–11, 2004), available Online at: «http://www.lesothoemb-usa.gov.ls/news/Hon.%20C.J.LEHOHLA%20SPEECH%20ROLE%20OF%20CUSTOMARY%20WASHINGTON%20JUNE%202004.doc» visited on October 21, 2006. See also generally A. Molokomme, "Reception and Development of Roman-Dutch Law in Botswana," *Lesotho Law Journal*, Vol. 1, (1985), p.121; E.K. Quansah, *Introduction to the Botswana Legal System*, (Gaborone: Pula Press, 2000); E.K. Quansah, "Educating Lawyers for Transnational Challenges: perspectives of a developing country," available Online at: «http://www.aals.org/international2004/Papers/quansahe.pdf», visited on October 21, 2006; and, Encyclopedia of Nations, "Zimbabwe: Judicial System," available Online at: «http://www.nationsencyclopedia.com/Africa/Zimbabwe-JUDICIAL-SYSTEM.html», visited on October 21, 2006.
3. See, for example, M.L. Lehohla, "The Role of Customary Law in Developing Africa: the Lesotho position," *Ibid*; A. Molokomme, "Reception and Development of Roman-Dutch Law in Botswana," *Ibid*; Encyclopedia of Nations, "Zimbabwe: Judicial System," *Ibid*; and, Legal Assistance Centre, "Summary of Proposals for Divorce Law Reform in Namibia," (June 2000), available Online at: «http://www.lac.org.na/grap/Pdf/divlawref-summ.pdf», visited on October 21, 2006.
4. P.F. Iya, "Legal Systems and Legal Education in Southern Africa: An Overview of Past Influences and Current Challenges," (Association of American Law Schools, 2000), available Online at: «http://www.aals.org/2000international/english/southafrica.htm», visited on October 21, 2006.
5. See *Ibid*.
6. See *Ibid*.
7. For example, P. Coutsoukis, "Swaziland-South Africa," extracted from *The Library of Congress Country Studies: CIA World Factbook*, available Online at:«http://www.photius.com/countries/south_africa/government/south_africa_government_swaziland.html», visited on October 21, 2006, observes: "In June 1993, South Africa and Swaziland signed a judicial agreement providing for

South African judges, magistrates, and prosecutors to serve in Swaziland's courts. South Africa also agreed to provide training for Swazi court personnel. In August 1995, the two countries signed an agreement to cooperate in anti-crime and anti-smuggling efforts along their common border."

8. Anonymous author, "Namibia: History," available Online at: «http://namibianhistory.com/», visited on October 21, 2006.
9. See M.Z. Booth, "Country Higher Education Profiles: Swaziland," INHEA, available Online at: «http://www.bc.edu/bc_org/avp/soe/cihe/inhea/profiles/Swaziland.htm», visited on October 21, 2006. See also generally D. Teferra and P.G. Altbach, (eds), *African Higher Education: An International Reference Handbook*, (Bloomington, IN: Indiana University Press, 2003); and, Jamboweb.com, "African Directory Online: Universities," available Online at: «http://www.jamboweb.com/drct/index.cfm?page_num=2&icat_id=12», visited on October 21, 2006. Also, according to the University of Pennsylvania Africa Studies Center, "Swaziland Page," available Online at: «http://www.africa.upenn.edu/Country_Specific/Swaziland.html», visited on October 21, 2006, "The University of Swaziland developed from the University of Botswana, Lesotho and Swaziland (UBLS), formerly known as the University of Basutoland, Bechuanaland and Swaziland (UBBS), which had its headquarters in Lesotho between 1964 and 1975. The UBBS had developed from the Pius XII Catholic University College at Roma (in Lesotho)."
10. Mindful, of course, that the US has a hierarchical order of specific professorships, such as assistant professor, associate professor, full professor, endowed Chair or distinguished professor and university professor.
11. See below.
12. Wikipedia, "Professor," available Online at: «http://en.wikipedia.org/wiki/Professor», visited on October 26, 2006.
13. See generally *Ibid.*
14. See generally *Ibid.*
15. See *Ibid.*
16. See R. Mukwena, "Crisis, Adjustment and Social Change in Zambia: the case of professionals," available Online at:«http://unpan1.un.org/intradoc/groups/public/documents/cafrad/unpan008090.pdf», visited on October 20, 2006.
17. See *Ibid.*
18. See *Ibid.*
19. Wikipedia, "Juris Doctor: History," available Online at:«http://en.wikipedia.org/wiki/Juris_Doctor», visited on October 21, 2006.
20. See *Ibid.*
21. J. Richardson, "Getting Into Law School—North America," *TriniNetwork.com* at: «http://www.trininetwork.com/news/lawart3.htm», visited in January 20, 2004.

22. See University of Toronto website, "Information About the JD Designation," at:«http://www.law.utoronto.ca/alumni_frnds_content.asp?itemPath=4/14/0/0/0&contentId=533&cType=webpages», visited on January 20, 2004.
23. See website of Chinese University of Hong Kong, "Juris Doctor Programme," at: «http://www.cuhk.edu.hk/law/jd.html», visited on October 21, 2006.
24. See website of Bond University, "Juris Doctor," at:«http://www.bond.edu.au/law/degrees/pg/jd.htm», visited on January 20, 2004.
25. See University of Melbourne website, "The Melbourne JD: a Unique Law Degree," at:«http://jd.unimelblaw.com.au/jdlaw.nsf», visited on January 20, 2004.
26. By contrast, some American law schools, such as Columbia University Law School, have chosen to collaborate with their UK counterparts to offer concurrently a dual law degree—that is, JD/LLB degree programme. For further insights into collaborative efforts of the University of Columbia Law School and the University of London colleges, see University of Columbia's website, "Columbia/University of London J.D./LL.B. Program," at: «http://www.law.columbia.edu/center_program/intl_progs/Double_degrees/JD_LLB», visited on January 20, 2004. The University of Detroit Mercy School of Law, in the US, and the University of Windsor, Faculty of Law, in Canada, have also established a joint dual degree programme, the JD/LLB degree programme. For further insights, see University of Detroit's website, "JD/LLB Program," at: «http://www.law.udmercy.edu/prospective/jdllb/applicationinfo.html», visited on January 20, 2004. On a similar note, the American University Law School in Washington DC has partnered with the University of Ottawa to offer a joint dual JD/LLB degree. For further insights into this programme, see American University's website, "JD/LL.B. Dual Degree Program: WCL—University of Ottawa," at: «http://www.wcl.american.edu/dualdegree/ottawa.cfm», visited on January 20, 2004. Furthermore, the American University Law School has forged other partnerships at postgraduate level to offer joint LLM degrees with the following universities abroad: the University of Makerere in Uganda, the University of Hull in the UK, City University of Hong Kong (which also offers a JD degree), Yonsei University College of Law in Korea, the University of Pretoria in South Africa, the University of the Western Cape in South Africa, and Erasmus University in the Netherlands. For fuller details on all these programmes, see American University's website, "Admissions," at: «http://www.wcl.american.edu/admiss/index.cfm», visited on January 20, 2004.
27. In general, the BJuris degree was offered either as part of the combined BJuris/LLB programme or an 'exit degree' for students who decided after admission not to proceed with an LLB degree. The BJuris, unlike the LLB degree, was not designed to provide a qualification for the professional practice of law. It provided a basic knowledge of law, an opportunity to study selected legal

courses of special interest, and significant study in other faculties. Various combinations of non-law courses were possible and the programme could be structured in a way that would meet various vocational ends, e.g., for industrial officers, public servants, business executives or law librarians. By contrast, the BProc was a four year undergraduate law degree.

28. Here, suffice it to say a discussion on the differences between the BJuris degree and the BProc degree is outside the scope of this study.
29. See N.Z. Makosana, "Accessing Higher Education in Apartheid South Africa: A Gender Perspective," *Jenda: A Journal of Culture and African Women Studies*, (2001), available Online at: «http://www.iiav.nl/ezines/web/JENda/Vol1(2000)Nr1/jendajournal/makosana.html», visited on October 21, 2006.
30. See *Ibid.*
31. This evident from the legal education curricula of most ABA accredited law schools in the US and, also, from the Bar admission requirements of different State Bars.
32. G. Pappas, "Re: the JD is not a Doctorate Degree," *The Mallet Street Gazette*, posting to an internet discussion forum, «http://www.malet.com/_ArticleFile/000000b8.htm», website visited on January 19, 2004.
33. O. Cromwell, "Re: JD is a first degree in law, not a graduate degree," *The Mallet Street Gazette*, posting to an internet discussion forum, «http://www.malet.com/_ArticleFile/000000b8.htm», website visited on January 19, 2004.
34. See *Ibid.*
35. See website of University of Ioannina, School of Medicine, "Academic Policies of the School of Medicine," at: «http://www.uoi.gr/schools/medschl/medicine/policie.html», visited on January 20, 2004.
36. See above and, also, below.
37. American Bar Association, Section of Legal Education and Admissions to the Bar, "Council Statements: J.D. Degree—Ph.D. Degree Equivalency," available Online at:«http://www.abanet.org/legaled/standards/councilstatements.html», visited on October 21, 2006.
38. See *Ibid.*
39. See US Department of Education, "First-Professional Studies: General Characteristics," available Online at: «http://www.ed.gov/about/offices/list/ous/international/usnei/us/edlite-professional-studies.html», visited on October 21, 2006.
40. See *Ibid.*
41. See website of Harvard University Law School, "Doctor of Juridical Science Program,"at:«http://www.law.harvard.edu/academics/graduate/programs/index.php», visited on January 20, 2004.

42. See website of Harvard University Law School, "Doctor of Juridical Science Program," at: «http://www.law.harvard.edu/academics/graduate/programs/index.php?page=sjd», visited on January 20, 2004.
43. See website of the University of Virginia Law School, "Academics: Degree Programs," at: «http://www.law.virginia.edu/home2002/html/academics/degree programs.htm», visited on January 20, 2004.
44. See *Ibid.*
45. See website of Pace University Law School, "Doctor of Juridical Science (S.J.D.)in Environmental Law," at: «http://www.law.pace.edu/environment/sjd2.html», visited on January 20, 2004.
46. See website of the International Centre for Legal Studies, "Frequently Asked Questions," at:«http://www.legaltutors.com/frequently_asked_questions.htm# What is an LL.B degree? Is it the same as the Juris Doctorate (JD) degree?», visited on January 20, 2004.
47. See website of University of Ioannina, School of Medicine, *op. cit.*
48. See *Ibid.*
49. On the need for most candidates applying for admission to a professional Doctorate programme to have some relevant practical experience, see T. Love, "Design-focused Professional Doctorates: Implications for Other Professional Doctoral Programs," at:«http://www.love.com.au/PublicationsTLminisite/2002/2002%20DesignFocusProdDoctorates_TL.htm», visited on January 21, 2004.
50. For an instructive report, see EIP, "Development Trends and Characteristics of Research-coursework Doctoral Programs," at:«http://www.detya.gov.au/archive/highered/eippubs/eip9707/chapter2.htm», visited on January 21, 2004.
51. See website of Queensland University of Technology, "Professional Doctorates," at: «http://www.appu.qut.edu.au/resources/profdoc.jsp», visited on January 21, 2004. See also R. Deem, "Doctoral routes—different paths to the same destination?" paper for the UK Council for Graduate Education Summer Conference, University of Greenwich, (1998, 15th-16th July); and, J.D. Nyquist, and B.J. Woodford, *Renvisioning the PhD- what concerns do we have?* (Washington: University of Washington, 2000).
52. E. M. Phillips and D.S. Pugh, *How to get a PhD*, (Buckingham: Open University Press, 1994), p. 181.
53. See E.M. Phillips and D.S. Pugh, *Ibid.*, p. 18.
54. See website of the University of Oxford Faculty of Law, "Oxford Law: Postgraduate taught courses, BCL" at: «http://denning.law.ox.ac.uk/postgraduate/bcl.shtml», visited on January 20, 2004.
55. See website of University of Columbia Law School, "Graduate Legal Studies," available Online at: «http://www.law.columbia.edu/llm_jsd/grad_studies», visited on October 24, 2006.

56. See below.
57. See website of KinsellaLaw.com, "'Doctor' Lawyer?", at: «http://www.kinsellalaw.com/archive/2002_04_01_archive.php» visited on January 20, 2004.
58. See *Ibid.*
59. See below for a fuller explanation of novel developments in Commonwealth Africa (e.g., at some law schools in Ghana, Zambia and South Africa), where some law schools are increasingly attracting candidates who already have an academic degree in another discipline to pursue the LLB degree. As stated below, even so, the status of this graduate-level LLB degree programme is not elevated above the status of the undergraduate version of the same degree. Both degrees have the same course content.
60. The only two exceptions here, pointing to the Americanisation of some academic programmes at law schools in Commonwealth countries, relate, first, to the adoption of a few courses from the curriculum of Master of Laws (LLM) degree programmes at some US law schools and, secondly, to the introduction of the American semester system at some universities in the Commonwealth.
61. The University of Ghana has embarked on a graduate LLB degree programme, attracting mainly candidates who already have an undergraduate degree in another field.
62. The University of Zambia (UNZA) Law School now runs a part-time LLB degree programme, with classes offered in the evenings. A good number of students on this LLB programme are, however, in full-time employment. Thus, they can only attend classes after work hours. And some of these students already have first degrees in other disciplines. From this crop of first degree holders, many failed initially, as undergraduates, to qualify into law school, ending up instead on less competitive undergraduate degree programmes before returning a few years later, as mature-age students, to campaign for a place in law school. At UNZA, like at many other universities in Commonwealth Africa, admission to law school, as an undergraduate, is intensely competitive. UNZA's experience with some mature-age graduate entrants into law school resembles that of the US where some aspiring and prospective law students, who fail to make it initially into law school, go on to pursue a PhD degree, say, in economics before returning to reapply for admission to the JD degree programme.
63. The University of Cape Town (UCT), for example, has a graduate LLB degree programme, attracting mainly candidates who already have an undergraduate degree in another field. For further details on this programme, see the following UCT web-site (i.e., under 'Law School', and then 'Degrees'): «http://www.uct.ac.za/», visited on October 22, 2006.
64. See the following untitled web-site of the National Law School of India:«http://www.paradygmlaw.com/nlsiu_bangalore.htm», visited on October 22, 2006.

65. With the possibility, of course, of permitting some candidates who wish to study law and who already hold a first degree in another discipline to take the first-professional degree in law as a graduate degree.
66. See generally Chapter 2 of this book.
67. American Bar Association, Section of Legal Education and Admissions to the Bar, "Overview of Post J.D. programs," available Online at:«http://www.abanet.org/legaled/postjdprograms/postjd.html», visited on October 21, 2006.
68. See below.
69. See American Bar Association, Section of Legal Education and Admissions to the Bar, "Overview of Post J.D. programs," *op. cit.*
70. See *Ibid.*
71. University of Columbia Law School, "Admissions Standards and Application Instructions: Graduates of All Other Law Schools," available Online at:«http://www.law.columbia.edu/llm_jsd/app_instr», visited on October 27, 2006.
72. See B. Leiter, "Information and Advice for Persons Interested in Teaching Law," (University of Texas, November 2002), available Online at: «http://www.utexas.edu/law/faculty/bleiter/GUIDE.HTM», visited on October 22, 2006.
73. See P. Cain and F. Pincus, "Faculty Fellowships Programs that lead to law teaching: Fellowships designed expressly to prepare future law professors," (University of Iowa, undated), available Online at: «http://www.law.arizona.edu/depts/chin/teachlaw/cainfellow.pdf», visited on October 22, 2006.
74. See *Ibid.*
75. See below.
76. See for example the admission requirements to Georgetown University Law Center's Graduate Fellowship Program for Future Law Professors as spelt out at: Georgetown University Law Center, "Graduate Fellowship Program for Future Law Professors," available Online at: «http://www.law.georgetown.edu/graduate/fellowships.html#3», visited on October 28, 2006.
77. See *Ibid.*
78. See the University of Kansas School of Law, "Full-Time Academic Openings: Stanford Law School—Legal Research and Writing Instructors," available Online at:«http://www.law.ku.edu/career_alumni/career_services/job_listing.shtml?31_full_time_academic», visited on October 28, 2006.
79. See the University of Kansas School of Law, "Full-Time Academic Openings: UCLA Law Teaching Fellowship," available Online at:«http://www.law.ku.edu/career_alumni/career_services/job_listing.shtml?31_full_time_academic», visited on October 28, 2006.
80. For example, a review of profiles of some current and former Associates in Law at Columbia University Law School shows that some foreign trained lawyers from

such developed countries as the UK, Germany, Australia, Israel and Canada have previously been admitted to the university's Associates in Law Program.

81. See B. Leiter, "Information and Advice for Persons Interested in Teaching Law," *op. cit.*
82. See *Ibid.*
83. See *Ibid.*
84. See website of Australia's La Trobe University, "Master of Laws (for international students)," at: «http://www.latrobe.edu.au/law/llm_int», visited on January 20, 2004.
85. An anonymous Nigerian's contribution to the BNW Forums and Message Board, "The Puerile Pastimes of Nd'Igbo" (February 11, 2002), available Online at:«http://messageboard.biafranigeriaworld.com/ultimatebb.cgi?ubb=get_topic&f=1&t=000575», visited on October 22, 2006.
86. See Chief Justice Randall T. Shepard, Chairperson of the Council of the Section of Legal Education and Admissions to the Bar of the American Bar Association, "Letter from Chairperson Shepard regarding post-JD programs," at«http://www.abanet.org/legaled/postjdprograms/postjd_letter.html», visited on January 21, 2004.
87. Worse still, an LLM degree from a foreign law school is, in many cases in the US, denied ample recognition. Yet, as explained above, both the American LLM and SJD degrees, unlike the JD, chronically suffer from lack of ABA accreditation.
88. See website of the University of Yale Law School, "The Degree of Doctor of the Science of Law (JSD)", at: «http://www.law.yale.edu/outside/html/Academics/acad-jsd.htm», visited on January 20, 2004. In the same manner, the University of Virginia Law School provides that: "The Law School also offers the Doctor of Juridical Science degree (SJD), the highest degree in law. Normally, a student is admitted to candidacy for the SJD *only after completing [the] LLM.* For foreign law graduates, the LLM programme is designed to provide both a broad introduction to American law and legal theory, and advanced training in specialised areas of the law that are relevant to the individual student's planned career in private practice, academics, or public service." See University of Virginia Law School, "LLM and SJD Programs," at:«http://www.law.virginia.edu/home2002/html/prospectives/grad/graduate.htm», visited on January 21, 2004.
89. See website of the University of Pennsylvania Law School, "Application for the SJD program," at: «http://www.law.upenn.edu/prospective/grad/apply/gplapplication.pdf», visited on January 21, 2004.
90. See *Ibid.*
91. Chief Justice Randall T. Shepard, Chairperson of the Council of the Section of Legal Education and Admissions to the Bar of the American Bar Association, *op. cit.*

92. See above.
93. See Chief Justice Randall T. Shepard, Chairperson of the Council of the Section of Legal Education and Admissions to the Bar of the American Bar Association, "Letter from Chairperson Shepard regarding post-JD programs," *op. cit.*
94. See *Ibid.*
95. See *Ibid.*
96. See *Ibid.*
97. See below.
98. Harvard Law School, "Graduate Program: Master of Laws (LLM) Program Overview," available Online at: «http://www.law.harvard.edu/academics/graduate/programs/llm.php», visited on October 22, 2006.
99. Universities UK observes, at: «http://www.universitiesuk.ac.uk/faqs/» visited on January 23, 2004: "There is no legal requirement that independent colleges are inspected or accredited; only voluntary schemes exist. There are two main independent accrediting bodies, the British Council (in the area of English as a Foreign Language) and the British Accreditation Council for Independent Further and Higher Education (BAC), which operate voluntary schemes of inspection and 'recognition'. However, of the 3,000 'college-type' institutions identified in the Department for Education survey, only some 350 institutions have chosen to be accredited in this way. The British Accreditation Council for Independent Further and Higher Education lists 100…"
100. See website of the Commonwealth Legal Education Association, "About the Commonwealth Legal Education Association (CLEA)," at: «http://www.uk-cle.ac.uk/clea/about/index.html»,visited on January 26, 2004.
101. Equally, the domestic bar associations of many Commonwealth African countries are not as pre-occupied with the accreditation of university academic law degrees as ABA.
102. See website of the British Academy, "Directory of UK Subject Associations and Learned Societies in the Humanities and Social Sciences," at:«http://www.britac.ac.uk/links/uksahssSections.asp?Section=S1», visited on January 26, 2004.
103. See website of the Commonwealth Legal Education Association, "About the Commonwealth Legal Education Association (CLEA)," *op. cit.*
104. See *Ibid.*
105. See *Ibid.*
106. See *Ibid.*
107. See *Ibid.*
108. See *Ibid.*
109. See *Ibid.*
110. See website of Association of American Law Schools, "What is the AALS," at«http://www.aals.org/about.html», visited on January 26, 2004.

111. See *Ibid.*
112. See *Ibid.*
113. See *Ibid.*
114. See website of the British Academy, "Directory of UK Subject Associations and Learned Societies in the Humanities and Social Sciences," *op. cit.*
115. See *Ibid.*
116. On the full list of members of the Association of African Universities, see website of the Association of African Universities, "Index of Member Universities," at:«http://www.aau.org/english/members.htm», visited on January 26, 2004.
117. See website of the Association of Commonwealth Universities, "Membership," at: «http://www.acu.ac.uk/cgi-bin/frameset.pl?ml=membership&sl=membership&select=members», visited on January 29, 2004.
118. See website of the Association of Commonwealth Universities, "History: About ACU," at:«http://www.acu.ac.uk/cgi-bin/frameset.pl?ml=aboutacu&sl=aboutacu&select=aboutacu», visited on January 29, 2004.
119. See *Ibid.*
120. See website of the Association of African Universities, "About AAU," at:«http://www.aau.org/english/aboutaau.htm», visited on January 26, 2004.
121. See *Ibid.*
122. See Wikipedia, "Private University," available Online at:«http://en.wikipedia.org/wiki/Private_university», visited on October 23, 2006.
123. See *Ibid.*
124. See Wikipedia, "School accreditation," available Online at:«http://en.wikipedia.org/wiki/School_accreditation», visited on October 23, 2006. Compared to the US, the UK has fewer accrediting bodies and these include such non-governmental and independent accrediting agencies as the British Accreditation Council.
125. See Wikipedia, "School accreditation," *Ibid.*
126. See for example Griffith University Act 1998, Southern Cross University Act 1993, Jawaharlal Nehru University Act 1966, Macquarie University Act 1989, York University Act, 1959, Calcutta University Act 1979, University of Waterloo Act 1972, and Bond University Act 1987.
127. D. Hawkins, the Executive Director of the Association of Canadian Medical Colleges, "Medical School Accreditation: A Canadian Case Study," at«http://www.fepafem.org.ve/david_h.htm», visited on January 24, 2004.
128. For example, as the Canadian Encyclopedia points out, "Encyclopedia of Music in Canada," at«http://www.canadianencyclopedia.ca/index.cfm?PgNm=TCE&ArticleId=U0002288», visited on January 23, 2004: "In 1813 James McGill, a prominent Montreal citizen and merchant, bequeathed £10,000 and a 18.4-hectare plot of land to the Royal Institution for the Advancement of Learning (established in 1801 to promote education in Lower

Canada) to found a college or university. In 1821 George IV granted a charter establishing the University of McGill College, a non-denominational institution. A reorganisation of the college was ratified by an 1852 charter, signed by Queen Victoria, and in 1885 the name was changed to McGill University. Courses began in 1829 in the Faculty of Medicine and in 1843 in the Faculty of Arts, the campus gradually expanding from its original location on the southeast side of Mount Royal. In 1990–1 McGill University comprised 12 faculties at the undergraduate level, a faculty of graduate studies and research (masters and doctorate degrees), 11 schools, and 4 incorporated or affiliated colleges, and some 2458 professors and 3803 non-professorial academic staff taught close to 30,000 students."

129. E.M. Phillips and D.S. Pugh, *How to get a PhD*, (Buckingham: Open University Press, 1994), p. 189.
130. The practice obtains at almost all major British universities.
131. See generally UK's Further and Higher Education Act 1992, which made changes in the funding and administration of further education and higher education in that country. A notable change introduced by this piece of legislation was to allow UK polytechnics to become universities. In addition the Act created bodies to fund higher education in England—the Higher Education Funding Council for England (HEFCE)—and further education—the Further Education Funding Council for England (FEFC).
132. See generally UK's Further and Higher Education Act 1992.
133. See for example Victoria University of Wellington, "Te Tohu Kairangi PhD," available Online at: «http://www.vuw.ac.nz/maori/degrees/doctor-of-philosophy.aspx», visited on October 23, 2006. See also University of Canterbury, "PhD Thesis Submission: Submission of a PhD thesis as a set of published research papers," available Online at:«http://www.anta.canterbury.ac.nz/courses/phd/phd_thesis_submission.shtml», visited on October 23, 2006.
134. See for example University of Monash Faculty of Law, "Guidelines for PhD theses by Publication," available Online at: «http://www.law.monash.edu.au/research/guidelines-phd-thesis-by-publication.pdf», visited on October 23, 2006.
135. See generally S. Powell, "The Award of PhD by Published Work in the UK," (UK Council for Graduate Education, 2004), available Online at:«http://www.ukcge.ac.uk/filesup/PhDbyPW.pdf», visited on October 23, 2006.
136. See S. Powell, *Ibid*, p. 39. See also K. Wilson, "Quality Assurance for a PhD by Published Work: a case study," *Quality Assurance in Education*, Vol. 10, No. 2 (2002), pp. 71–78.
137. See the web-site of University of Columbia Law School, "J.S.D Program: Doctor of the Science of Law (J.S.D.) Degree," available Online at:«http://www.law.columbia.edu/llm_jsd/jsd», visited on October 24, 2006.

138. See the web-site of University of Pennsylvania Law School, "Degree Requirements: The Doctor of Juridical Science Degree (SJD)," available Online at:«http://www.law.upenn.edu/registrar/requirements.html#sjd», visited on October 24, 2006.

139. For example, Lund University in Sweden points out that: (see web-site of Lund University at: «http://www.lu.se/o.o.i.s/1665», visited on October 27, 2006): "Ph.D. programmes are offered within most of the traditional university disciplines… The Ph.D program normally consists of two parts: courses and thesis." And the African Economic Research Consortium, an African regional body awarding fellowships for doctoral studies in economics to qualifying African students, points out that (see web-site of the African Economic Research Consortium «http://www.aercafrica.org/programmes/training_cpp.asp», visited on October 30, 2006): "*Universities Participating in the Collaborative PhD Programme*: All universities in sub-Saharan Africa are eligible to participate in the programme. Through a series of stakeholders 'meetings spanning from June 2001 to May 2002, it was agreed that the universities be classified into three groups:

(a) *Host Degree-Awarding Universities*: These are the universities that have been assigned the responsibility of teaching courses in core fields. For purposes of implementing the programme, the continent is subdivided into four regions, Southern Africa, Eastern Africa, Anglophone West Africa and Francophone Africa. There is, to start with, one host degree-awarding university per region. The universities are:

- University of Cape Town for Southern Africa
- University of Dar es Salaam for Eastern Africa
- University of Ibadan for Anglophone West Africa
- University of Yaounde II for Francophone Africa

(b) *Non-Host Degree-awarding universities (DAUs)*: These are the additional universities charged with the responsibility of awarding PhD degrees in economics to students who fulfil all the requirements for the award of the degree under the programme. The DAUs admit students on the basis of agreed criteria, send the students to the regional host universities to take core courses and thereafter to a central facility—the Joint Facility for Electives (JFE)—to take elective courses, organize the supervision and production of student PhD theses (including allowing students and their supervisors to attend PhD workshops), and award the degrees to successful students. The following universities are categorized as non-host degree-awarding universities:

- University of Witwatersrand (South Africa)
- University of Nairobi (Kenya)
- University of Benin (Nigeria)
- University of Cocody (Abidjan)

As stated above, the host DAUs organize the teaching on courses in core fields on a regional basis. The major difference between host and non-host DAUs is that the former teach core courses and conduct comprehensive examinations, which functions the latter does not perform. All the 8 DAUs award PhD degrees to students who will fulfill the agreed requirements."

140. See Wikipedia, "Higher Doctorates in the United Kingdom, Ireland and the Commonwealth," available Online at:«http://en.wikipedia.org/wiki/Doctorate#Higher_Doctorates_in_the_United_Kingdom.2C_Ireland_and_the_Commonwealth», visited on October 24, 2006.
141. See *Ibid.*
142. See above and, also, below.
143. See below.
144. See Wikipedia, "Doctor of Laws," available Online at:«http://en.wikipedia.org/wiki/Doctor_of_Laws», visited on October 24, 2006.
145. (Material in this footnote is not part of the quotation and is my own emphasis) Except for universities such as the University of Cape Town, the University of Witwatersrand and Rhodes University which offer a separate programme for the PhD in Law while making provision also the higher Doctorate in law (the LLD degree).
146. See Wikipedia, "Doctor of Laws," *op. cit.*
147. Institute of Higher Education, Shanghai Jiao Tong University, "Ranking Methodology: Ranking Criteria and Weights," available Online at:«http://ed.sjtu.edu.cn/rank/2006/ARWU2006Methodology.htm», visited on October 30, 2006.
148. K. Leyn, "Ranking Universities," available Online at: «http://www.freewebtown.com/lyen/rankingu.html», visited on October 29, 2006.
149. See *Ibid.*
150. See *Ibid.*
151. American Bar Association, Section of Legal Education and Admissions to the Bar, "Council Statements: Rating of Law Schools," available Online at:«http://www.abanet.org/legaled/standards/councilstatements.html», visited on October 21, 2006.
152. See generally M. Zawel, *Untangling the Ivy League*, (Pittsburgh, PA: College Prowler, 2005); and, M.A. Hernández, *A Is for Admission: The Insider's Guide to Getting into the Ivy League and Other Top Colleges*, (New York, NY: Warner Books, 1999).

153. See Princeton University's websites, "Ivy League," at: «http://etc.princeton.edu/CampusWWW/Companion/ivy_league.html», visited on January 22, 2004.
154. See *Ibid.*
155. See Wikipedia Encyclopedia, "Russell Group of Universities," at: «http://en2.wikipedia.org/wiki/Russell_Group_of_Universities», visited on January 22, 2004.
156. See *Ibid.*
157. See University of Cambridge, News Cuttings Archive (extracted from *Times newspaper*, Tuesday, May 18, 2004, p. 9), "Oxbridge dominates academic league tables," available Online at: «http://www.admin.cam.ac.uk/news/daily/archive.cgi?1084748400», visited on October 30, 2006.
158. See P. Curtis, "Subsidising students is economic folly," in *Guardian newspaper*, June 28, 2002, available Online at:«http://education.guardian.co.uk/specialreports/tuitionfees/story/0,5500,746017,00.html», visited on October 30, 2006.
159. As quoted by F. Sabatini (ed), (University of Rome La Sapienza and University of Cassino), "Social Capital Gateway: Resources for the Study of Social Capital," extracting university rankings from the web-site of InternetLab (*Observatorio de Ciencia y Tecnologia en Internet*). The article containing the said ranking of African universities is available Online at: «http://www.socialcapitalgateway.org/eng-rankingafrica.htm», visited on October 29, 2006.
160. Registered initially as an MPhil student before being confirmed, a year later, to the status of a PhD student.

Bibliography

African Economic Research Consortium (Online, retrieved October 30, 2006), 'Training—collaborative PhD programme (CPP) in economics,' Available at: «http://www.aercafrica.org/programmes/training_cpp.asp»

American Bar Association, Section of Legal Education and Admissions to the Bar (Online, retrieved October 21, 2006), 'Council statements: J.D. degree—Ph.D. degree equivalency,' Available at: «http://www.abanet.org/legaled/standards/councilstatements.html»

American Bar Association, Section of Legal Education and Admissions to the Bar (Online, retrieved October 21, 2006), 'Council statements: Rating of law schools,' Available at: «http://www.abanet.org/legaled/standards/councilstatements.html»

American Bar Association, Section of Legal Education and Admissions to the Bar (Online, retrieved October 21, 2006), 'Overview of post J.D. programs,' Available at: «http://www.abanet.org/legaled/postjdprograms/postjd.html»

American University (Online, retrieved January 20, 2004), 'Admissions,' Available at: «http://www.wcl.american.edu/admiss/index.cfm»

American University (Online, retrieved January 20, 2004), 'JD/LL.B. dual degree program: WCL—University of Ottawa,' Available at: «http://www.wcl.american.edu/dualdegree/ottawa.cfm»

Anonymous author (Online, retrieved October 21, 2006), 'Namibia: History,' Available at: «http://namibianhistory.com»

An anonymous contribution to the BNW Forums and Message Board (Online, retrieved October 22, 2006), 'The puerile pastimes of Nd'Igbo' (February 11, 2002), Available at: «http://messageboard.biafranigeriaworld.com/ultimatebb.cgi?ubb=get_topic&f=1&t=000575»

Association of African Universities (Online, retrieved January 26, 2004), 'About AAU,' Available at: «http://www.aau.org/english/aboutaau.htm»

Association of American Law Schools (Online, retrieved January 26, 2004), 'What is the AALS,' Available at: «http://www.aals.org/about.html»

Association of Commonwealth Universities (Online, retrieved January 29, 2004), 'Membership,' Available at: «http://www.acu.ac.uk/cgi-bin/frameset.pl?ml=membership&sl=membership&select=members»

Bond University (Online retrieved January 20, 2004), 'Juris Doctor,' Available at: «http://www.bond.edu.au/law/degrees/pg/jd.htm»

Booth, M. Z. (Online, retrieved October 21, 2006), 'Country higher education profiles: Swaziland,' Available at: «http://www.bc.edu/bc_org/avp/soe/cihe/inhea/profiles/Swaziland.htm»

British Academy (Online, retrieved January 26, 2004), 'Directory of UK Subject Associations and Learned Societies in the Humanities and Social Sciences,' Available at: «http://www.britac.ac.uk/links/uksahssSectionsasp?Section=S1»

Cain, P. and Pincus, F. (Online, retrieved October 22, 2006), 'Faculty fellowships programs that lead to law teaching: Fellowships designed expressly to prepare future law professors' (University of Iowa, undated), Available at: «http://www.law.arizona.edu/depts/chin/teachlaw/cainfellow.pdf»

Canadian Encyclopedia (Online, retrieved January 23, 2004), 'Encyclopedia of Music in Canada,' Available at: «http://www.canadianencyclopedia.ca/index.cfm?PgNm=TCE&ArticleId=U0002288»

Chinese University of Hong Kong (Online, retrieved October 21, 2006), 'Juris Doctor Programme,' Available at: «http://www.cuhk.edu.hk/law/jd.html»

Commonwealth Legal Education Association (Online, retrieved January 26, 2004), 'About the Commonwealth Legal Education Association (CLEA),' Available at: «http://www.ukcle.ac.uk/clea/about/index.html»

Chief Justice Randall T. Shepard, Chairperson of the Council of the Section of Legal Education and Admissions to the Bar of the American Bar Association (Online, retrieved January 21, 2004), 'Letter from Chairperson Shepard regarding post-JD programs,' Available at: «http://www.abanet.org/legaled/postjdprograms/postjd_letter.html»

Coutsoukis, P. (Online, retrieved October 21, 2006), 'Swaziland–South Africa,' Available at: «http://www.photius.com/countries/south_africa/government/south_africa_government_swaziland.html»

Cromwell, O. (Online, retrieved January 19, 2004), 'Re: JD is a first degree in law, not a graduate degree,' *The Mallet Street Gazette*, Available at: «http://www.malet.com/_ArticleFile/000000b8.htm»

Curtis, P. (2002), 'Subsidising students is economic folly,' *Guardian,*28 June (Online, retrieved October 30, 2006), Available at: «http://education.guardian.co.uk/specialreports/tuitionfees/story/ 0,5500,746017,00.html»

Deem, R. (1998, 15–16 July), 'Doctoral routes—Different paths to the same destination?' Paper for the UK Council for Graduate Education Summer Conference, University of Greenwich.

EIP (Online, retrieved January 21, 2004), 'Development trends and characteristics of research-coursework doctoral programs,' Available at: «http://www.detya.gov.au/archive/highered/eippubs/eip9707/chapter2.htm»

Encyclopedia of Nations (Online, retrieved October 21, 2006), 'Zimbabwe: Judicial system,' Available at: «http://www.nationsencyclopedia.com/Africa/Zimbabwe-JUDICIAL-SYSTEM.html»

Georgetown University Law Center (Online, retrieved October 28, 2006), 'Graduate Fellowship Program for Future Law Professors,' Available at: «http://www.law.georgetown.edu/graduate/fellowships.html#3»

Harvard University Law School (Online, retrieved October 22, 2006), 'Graduate Program: Master of Laws (LLM) Program Overview,' Available at: «http://www.law.harvard.edu/academics/graduate/programs/llm.php»

Harvard University Law School (Online, retrieved January 20, 2004), 'Doctor of Juridical Science Program,' Available at: «http://www.law.harvard.edu/academics/graduate/programs/index.php»

Hawkins, D., the Executive Director of the Association of Canadian Medical Colleges (Online, retrieved January 24, 2004), 'Medical School Accreditation: A Canadian Case Study,' Available at: «http://www.fepafem.org.ve/david_h.htm»

Hernández, M. A. (1999), *A Is for Admission: The Insider's Guide to Getting into the Ivy League and Other Top Colleges*, Warner Books, New York.

International Centre for Legal Studies (Online, retrieved January 20, 2004), 'Frequently asked questions,' Available at: «http://www.legaltutors.com/frequently_asked_questions.htm#What is an LL.B degree? Is it the same as the Juris Doctorate (JD) degree?»

Institute of Higher Education, Shanghai Jiao Tong University (Online, retrieved October 30, 2006), 'Ranking methodology: Ranking criteria and weights,' Available at: «http://ed.sjtu.edu.cn/rank/2006/ARWU2006Methodology.htm»

Iya, P. F. (Online, retrieved October 21, 2006), 'Legal systems and legal education in Southern Africa: An overview of past influences and current challenges,' Available at: «http://www.aals.org/2000international/english/southafrica htm»

Jamboweb.com (Online, retrieved October 21, 2006), 'African Directory Online: Universities,' Available at: «http://www.jamboweb.com/drct/index.cfm?page_num=2&icat_id=12»

KinsellaLaw.com (Online, retrieved January 20, 2004), '"Doctor" lawyer?' Available at: «http://www.kinsellalaw.com/archive/2002_04_01_archive.php»

La Trobe University (Online, retrieved January 20, 2004), 'Master of Laws (for international students),' Available at: «http://www.latrobe.edu.au/law/llm_int»

Legal Assistance Centre (Online, retrieved October 21, 2006), 'Summary of proposals for Divorce Law Reform in Namibia,' Available at: «http://www.lac.org.na/grap/Pdf/divlawref-summ.pdf»

Lehohla, M. L. (Online, retrieved October 21, 2006), 'The role of customary law in developing Africa: The Lesotho position' (Washington, DC: July 9–11, 2004), Available at: «http://www.lesothoemb-usa.gov.ls/news/Hon.%20C.J.LEHOHLA%20SPEECH%20ROLE%20OF%20CUSTOMARY%20WASHINGTON%20JUNE%202004.doc»

Leiter, B. (Online, retrieved October 22, 2006), 'Information and advice for persons interested in teaching law' (University of Texas, November 2002), Available at: «http://www.utexas.edu/law/faculty/bleiter/GUIDE.HTM»

Leyn, K. (Online, retrieved October 29, 2006), 'Ranking universities,' Available at: «http://www.freewebtown.com/lyen/rankingu.html»

Love, T. (Online, retrieved January 21, 2004), 'Design-focused professional doctorates: Implications for other professional doctoral programs,' Available at: «http://www.love.com.au/PublicationsTLminisite/2002/2002%20DesignFocusProdDoctorates_TL.htm»

Lund University (Online, retrieved October 27, 2006), 'PhD programmes,' Available at: «http://www.lu.se/o.o.i.s/1665»

Makosana, N. Z. (Online, retrieved October 21, 2006), 'Accessing higher education in apartheid South Africa: A gender perspective,' *Jenda: A Journal of Culture and African Women Studies*, Available at: «http://www.iiav.nl/ezines/web/JENda/Vol1(2000)Nr1/jendajournal/makosana.html»

Molokomme, A. (1985), 'Reception and development of Roman–Dutch law in Botswana,' *Lesotho Law Journal*, vol. 1, p. 121.

Mukwena, R. (Online, retrieved October 20, 2006), 'Crisis, adjustment and social change in Zambia: The case of professionals,' Available at: «http://unpan1.un.org/intradoc/groups/public/documents/cafrad/unpan008090.pdf»

National Law School of India (Online, retrieved October 22, 2006), Untitled website, Available at: «http://www.paradygmlaw.com/nlsiu_bangalore.htm»

Nyquist, J. D. and Woodford, B. J. (2000), Re-envisioning the PhD—what concerns do we have? University of Washington, Washington.

Pace University Law School (Online, retrieved January 20, 2004), 'Doctor of juridical science (S.J.D.) in Environmental Law,' Available at «http://www.law.pace.edu/environment/sjd2.html»

Pappas, G. (Online, retrieved January 19, 2004), 'Re: the JD is not a doctorate degree,' *The Mallet Street Gazette*, Available at: «http://www.malet.com/_ArticleFile/000000b8.htm»

Phillips, E. M. and Pugh, D. S. (1994), *How to Get a PhD*, Open University Press, Buckingham, UK.

Powell, S. (Online, retrieved October 23, 2006), 'The award of PhD by published work in the UK' (UK Council for Graduate Education, 2004), Available at: «http://www.ukcge.ac.uk/filesup/PhDbyPW.pdf»

Princeton University (Online, retrieved January 22, 2004), 'Ivy League,' Available at: «http://etc.princeton.edu/CampusWWW/Companion/ivy_league.html»

Quansah, E. K. (2000), *Introduction to the Botswana Legal System*, Pula Press, Gaborone, Botswana, South Africa.

Quansah, E. K. (Online retrieved October 21, 2006), 'Educating lawyers for transnational challenges: Perspectives of a developing country,' Available at: «http://www.aals.org/international2004/Papers/quansahe.pdf»

Queensland University of Technology (Online, retrieved January 21, 2004), 'Professional doctorates,' Available at «http://www.appu.qut.edu.au/resources/profdoc.jsp»

Richardson, J. (Online, retrieved January 20, 2004), 'Getting into law school—North America,' *TriniNetwork.com,* Available at: «http://www.trininetwork.com/news/lawart3.htm»

Sabatini, F. (ed) (Online, retrieved October 29, 2006), 'Social capital gateway: Resources for the study of social capital,' Available at: «http://www.socialcapitalgateway.org/eng-rankingafrica.htm»

Teferra, D. and Altbach, P. G. (eds) (2003), *African Higher Education: An International Reference Handbook*, Indiana University Press, Bloomington, IN.

University of Cambridge (Online, retrieved October 30, 2006), 'Oxbridge dominates academic league tables,' Available at: «http://www.admin.cam.ac.uk/news/daily/archive.cgi?1084748400»

University of Canterbury (Online, retrieved October 23, 2006), 'PhD thesis submission: Submission of a PhD thesis as a set of published research papers,' Available at: «http://www.anta.canterbury.ac.nz/courses/phd/phd_thesis_submission.shtml»

University of Cape Town (Online, retrieved October 22, 2006), 'Faculty of Law,' Available at: «http://www.uct.ac.za»

University of Columbia (Online, retrieved January 20, 2004), 'Columbia/University of London J.D./LL.B. Program,' Available at: «http://www.law.columbia.edu/center_program/intl_progs/Double_degrees/JD_LLB»

University of Columbia Law School (Online, retrieved October 27, 2006), 'Admissions standards and application instructions: Graduates of all other law schools,' Available at: «http://www.law.columbia.edu/llm_jsd/app_instr»

University of Columbia Law School (Online, retrieved October 24, 2006), 'Graduate legal studies,' Available at: «http://www.law.columbia.edu/llm_jsd/grad_studies»

University of Columbia Law School (Online, retrieved October 24, 2006), 'J.S.D Program: Doctor of the Science of Law (J.S.D.) Degree,' Available at: «http://www.law.columbia.edu/llm_jsd/jsd»

University of Detroit (Online, retrieved January 20, 2004), 'JD/LLB Program,' Available at: «http://www.law.udmercy.edu/prospective/jdllb/applicationinfo.html»

University of Ioannina, School of Medicine (Online, retrieved January 20, 2004), 'Academic policies of the School of Medicine,' Available at: «http://www.uoi.gr/schools/medschl/medicine/policie.html»

University of Kansas School of Law (Online, retrieved October 28, 2006), 'Full-time academic openings: Stanford Law School—legal research and writing instructors,' Available at: «http://www.law.ku.edu/career_alumni/career_services/job_listing.shtml?31_full_time_academic»

University of Kansas School of Law (Online, retrieved October 28, 2006), 'Full-time academic openings: UCLA Law Teaching Fellowship,' Available at: «http://www.law.ku.edu/career_alumni/career_services/job_listing.shtml?31_full_time_academic»

University of Melbourne (Online, retrieved January 20, 2004), 'The Melbourne JD: A unique law degree,' Available at: «http://jd.unimelblaw.com.au/jdlaw.nsf»

University of Monash Faculty of Law (Online, retrieved October 23, 2006), 'Guidelines for PhD theses by publication,' Available at: «http://www.law.monash.edu.au/research/guidelines-phd-thesis-by-publication.pdf»

University of Oxford Faculty of Law (Online, retrieved January 20, 2004), 'Oxford Law: Postgraduate taught courses, BCL,' Available at: «http://denning.law.ox.ac.uk/postgraduate/bcl.shtml»

University of Pennsylvania Law School (Online, retrieved January 21, 2004), 'Application for the SJD program,' Available at: «http://www.law.upenn.edu/prospective/grad/apply/gplapplication.pdf»

University of Pennsylvania Law School (Online, retrieved October 24, 2006), 'Degree requirements: The Doctor of Juridical Science Degree (SJD),' Available at: «http://www.law.upenn.edu/registrar/requirements.html#sjd»

University of Pennsylvania Africa Studies Center (Online, retrieved October 21, 2006), 'Swaziland Page,' Available at: «http://www.africa.upenn.edu/Country_Specific/Swaziland.html»

University of Toronto (Online, retrieved January 20, 2004), 'Information about the JD designation,' Available at: «http://www.law.utoronto.ca/alumni_frnds_content.asp?itemPath=4/14/0/0/0&contentId=533&cType=webpages»

Universities UK (Online, retrieved January 23, 2004), Available at: «http://www.universitiesuk.ac.uk/faqs»

University of Virginia Law School (Online, retrieved January 20, 2004), 'Academics: Degree programs,' Available at: «http://www.law.virginia.edu/home2002/html/academics/degreeprograms.htm»

University of Virginia Law School (Online, retrieved January 21, 2004), 'LLM and SJD programs,' Available at: «http://www.law.virginia.edu/home2002/html/prospectives/grad/graduate.htm»

University of Yale Law School (Online, retrieved January 20, 2004), 'The Degree of Doctor of the Science of Law (JSD)', Available at: «http://www.law.yale.edu/outside/html/Academics/acad-jsd.htm»

US Department of Education (Online, retrieved October 21, 2006), 'First-professional studies: General characteristics,' Available at: «http://www.ed.gov/about/offices/list/ous/international/usnei/us/edlite-professional-studies.html»

Victoria University of Wellington (Online, retrieved October 23, 2006), 'Te Tohu Kairangi PhD,' Available at: «http://www.vuw.ac.nz/maori/degrees/doctor-of-philosophy.aspx»

Wikipedia Encyclopedia (Online, retrieved October 24, 2006), 'Doctor of Laws,' Available at: «http://en.wikipedia.org/wiki/Doctor_of_Laws»

Wikipedia Encyclopedia (Online, retrieved October 24, 2006), 'Higher Doctorates in the United Kingdom, Ireland and the Commonwealth,' Available at: «http://en.wikipedia.org/wiki/Doctorate#Higher_Doctorates_in_the_United_Kingdom.2C_Ireland_and_the_Commonwealth»

Wikipedia Encyclopedia (Online, retrieved October 21, 2006), 'Juris Doctor: History,' Available at: «http://en.wikipedia.org/wiki/Juris_Doctor»

Wikipedia Encyclopedia (Online, retrieved October 23, 2006), 'Private university,' Available at: «http://en.wikipedia.org/wiki/Private_university»

Wikipedia Encyclopedia (Online, retrieved October 26, 2006), 'Professor,' Available at: «http://en.wikipedia.org/wiki/Professor»

Wikipedia Encyclopedia (Online, retrieved January 22, 2004), 'Russell Group of Universities,' Available at: «http://en2.wikipedia.org/wiki/Russell_Group_of_Universities»

Wikipedia Encyclopedia (Online, retrieved October 23, 2006), 'School accreditation,' Available at: «http://en.wikipedia.org/wiki/School_accreditation»

Wilson, K. (2002), 'Quality assurance for a PhD by published work: A case study,' *Quality Assurance in Education*, vol. 10, no. 2, p. 71–78.

Zawel, M. *(2005), Untangling the Ivy League,* College Prowler, Pittsburgh, PA.

Index

Made in the USA
Monee, IL
12 November 2026

537ab7a4-faff-4593-8c3f-e39348a2c716R01